THE INVISIBLE
CLARINETIST

THE INVISIBLE CLARINETIST

Joe Licari

To order additional copies of this book, contact:
Xlibris Corporation
1-888-795-4274
www.Xlibris.com
Orders@Xlibris.com
24147

CONTENTS

DEDICATION

Dedicated to my wife, Valerie, who put up with so much during my musical life and allowed me to do what I loved most, playing music. And to my children. Theresa, John, Marian, Francis, David, Dominic, Ann, Joseph, Jr., Michael, and Paul. I wrote this book for you so you can see what my life was like before and while all of you were growing up.

I'm sorry for any of my neglect during all those years, but you all turned out well in spite of me.,

ACKNOWLEDGEMENTS

A special thank you to Dick Roberts a long time friend, for giving me the encouragement to write this book. Dick is the author of "Boathouse Days" published by Xlibris, and a Teacher, Musician and Screenwriter. Also, John Maimone who did all the re-typing of the manuscript and editing. John worked in radio broadcasting, studio and location recording of jazz and he loves our kind of music.

Also, to Bob Wilber who was gracious enough to write the Forward for this book. Bob is internationally renowned as a clarinetist, saxophonist, arranger, and has won a Grammy Award for his work on Coppola's hit movie, "The Cotton Club." He is also author of "Music Was Not Enough." He is a long time friend and life time Mentor.

Thanks, also, to the following who contributed in some way: Barbara and Dick Dreiwitz, Natalie Lamb, David Ostwald, Cynthia Sayer, Red Balaban, Ida Moore, Joe H. Klee and Dick Voigt. Some of the material is from radio interviews from The Jim Lowe Show and from my personal correspondence from cards and letters from musicians.

PREFACE

I call myself The Invisible Clarinetist, as I never really achieved the kind of fame or notoriety I might have liked. This story is about my musical life and about some of the people who have come to share and enrich it. Music has always been my first love but my wife and family of ten children had to be my first priority, and raising ten kids is another book all by itself.

This book celebrates my musical life as I lived it. This accountability, as I call it, is dedicated and intended for my children, so they know how hard I had to work to support them and accounted for why I wasn't around much while they were growing up. I had to work day jobs plus playing the music at night so I wasn't around much. I guess if I was to blame someone for what some people might call neglect, or child abuse, it would have to be Benny Goodman the great Chicago jazz clarinetist. I heard an early recording of Benny with the Ben Pollack band and fell in love with his hot playing. I maintain that Goodman did his best playing around that period between 1926 to 1934. But that's my opinion.

I knew that I had to have a clarinet and approached my father and he got me my first metal clarinet. With lots of practice and lots of playing over the years I think I have become a good player. I also think I was born at the wrong time as if it were ten or more years earlier I might have made a name for myself playing with all those great musicians who came before me. But I'll never know now and shouldn't dwell on what did not happen, but on what did happen.

I have been blessed to have played with some great musicians as you will discover in the book and have made good friends and associations during the past 50 years. I still look forward to playing and the enjoyment of my playing the music I love has kept me feeling young and happy. What more can one ask for?

If I had to do it all over again, I probably would do it the same way.

FORWARD

Walking past the post office in the little country town in England where Pug and I live, I espied a sign in the window along with notices of lost dogs, bake sales, cleaning women needed, etc. It read, Learn to play jazz—it's fun and it's easy!

I was tempted to ring the phone number listed. Having worked at playing jazz for fifty-seven years (fun, sometimes, but definitely not easy), I figured there must be some magic formula which I never knew about!

Suffice to say a life dedicated to playing jazz can be difficult and in economic terms un-rewarding. If one is into classic jazz (i.e., the music before the advent of be-bop in the 1940's) there are other obstacles: The jazz media (critics, major record companies, jazz on radio, TV, etc.) seem to be perpetually chasing the latest fad, desparate to be on the bandwagon of the newest jazz genius.

Wynton Marsalis put the case for classic jazz succinctly: "We're coming now into the time that the earliest jazz fits. This is the time of King Oliver and Jelly Roll Morton. For our music we don't have to keep inventing the wheel that we invented already. What we have to do is learn to play it!"

This lengthy preamble is my way of introducing you to Joe Licari. Joe has spent the major part of his life learning to play classic jazz, studying the whole history of the music via recordings and hearing some of the early masters in person. You hear the influence of Benny Goodman in his playing (how can one avoid it?), but also the Chicago players Frank Teschemacher and Pee Wee Russell plus the New Orleans clarinetists Dodds, Bechet and Noone.

He has used some of their ideas and rejected others to come up with his own style. When you hear Joe's clarinet you know it's him. To achieve this identity is the goal of all serious players.

I'm sure my friend Joe would agree with me: The sign in the post office window got it wrong. A career in jazz can be fun, but easy it's not!

Bob Wilber—Chipping Campden, England

CHAPTER ONE

Early Childhood (Growing up)

I was born Joseph Licari on January 10, 1934 at Cumberland Hospital in Brooklyn. Seventeen days later I was baptized at St. Lucy's Church on Kent Avenue.

Mom and Pop came to America from Italy around 1920. My Pop was born in Palermo, Sicily, and my Mom was from the Province of Trapani. Upon docking in New York City they found a place in Brooklyn and settled there. Pop's first job here was working for the WPA.

As life went on they were blessed with five children. Jeanne was the oldest, then my older brother Rocco who had been the chubbiest of all us kids at birth, we were told. Next came Andrew and then myself who was always considered by Mom as the baby of the boys. Finally, we have a real baby of the family, my sister Marie. Although we were a poor family Pop had always worked hard to do his best for us.

My earliest recollection was at the age of six and the peculiar situations I would get myself into. There was an old abandoned building on our street and a few of us kids would sneak off and play there. One day while playing in this old building one of the kids was playing with matches and something caught fire. We all got out of there in a hurry. Then the fire engines came to put the fire out. We kids looked on in excitement not fully realizing that we were the cause of it. I never mentioned it to Mom as I would get the belt across my fanny.

We lived in a tenement building three flights up and I was always sliding down the bannister. One day while playing I fell off the bannister and down the stairs I went. With my luck, I didn't miss a step. The result was a cut on my head and a broken leg.

Being in a cast the next few weeks wasn't so bad as everyone was treating me nice and catering to my every need. Gustav, my Godfather, came to visit me often and always brought me candy or ice cream. He would carry me down three flights of stairs to our front stoop so I could watch the other kids playing in the street. Upon seeing me, the kids would gather around to look at my cast and autograph it. I think they were a bit envious of me as I was getting all this attention. All good things come to an end as finally my cast came off and that was the end of that.

My next oldest brother, Andrew, was supposed to be taking care of me but was nowhere to be found. I found myself in the street and a car which had stopped quickly upon seeing me tapped me gently from behind with its fender. I cried a little but I wasn't hurt. The driver was more scared than I was. He kept asking me in a nervous sort of way if I was okay. My brother arrived on the scene just in time as the man, who was trying desperately to have us forget the incident, took us down to the corner drug store for ice cream sodas.

It was now around 1940 and my oldest brother, Rocky, had just graduated high school and not really knowing what he wanted to do, like most young men at that time, went away to CCC camp.

Not too long after that we moved to a small town in South Jersey called Vineland. It was a nice town and the country air smelled so fresh and clean. Compared to Brooklyn this was a paradise. We already had my aunt and uncle and cousins living here. I guess my parents left the city so we could all be together. Pop got a job at the local power plant and rented a small house for us not far from town.

My parents immediately enrolled me in a parochial school called the Sacred Heart. I started in the second grade. I can still remember my first teacher who was a petit nun named, Sister Dolores. She was pretty and had the face of a saint. I liked all the nuns there and they seemed to like me. It could be because it was easy to get me to stay after school to help clean the blackboards and close the transoms.

When I was in the sixth grade and about 12 years of age, I had my first encounter with music. It seems the music teacher, Sister Anita Gertrude, needed a few boys to learn how to play these six-holed red plastic whistles. Although it appeared to be toy-like it was capable of making nice music, as I was to find out.

Being exposed to this instrument I found, before long, that I had a good ear for music and learned to play songs on it quite easily. The music teacher was preparing us for an upcoming recital and taught us how to play, Carnival of Venice. The big night of the recital came and it went very well. Sister Anita was very proud of us. She was a major influence in my life, getting me interested in music and always encouraging me to take up an instrument. It was years later, at age 16, that I took up the clarinet.

One day I discovered that my sister, Jeanne, had this collection of 78's which included swing bands and singers. I listened to this one recording of the Benny Goodman band and remember how it excited me. I knew then that I wanted to play a clarinet. I asked Pop, and although he couldn't afford it he said he would see what he could do. I realize, now that I'm older, how he sacrificed his own needs to please us.

A few days later he took me down to the local music store which was just a few blocks from our house. He introduced me to the owner that everyone called, Spike. Spike played the trumpet in local club date bands and gave lessons. He went behind the counter and took out this clarinet case, and opened it. Inside was a shiny metal clarinet which he said was a good beginner's instrument. Pop made arrangements to give him a few bucks a week till it was paid off. It felt great having my own instrument and I couldn't wait to get home and fool with it.

I didn't get clarinet lessons right away but with a lot of practice and experimentation I managed to get a decent tone and learned to play by ear. I was able to hear a tune and find it on my horn. Now the fun was beginning. I now was ready for lessons and found a good teacher by the name of Bob MaGarry. He taught at a music store in town. He was considered a good reed player and played in some local groups. He taught me how to read well enough to get by. He would give me lessons out of a Klose Method clarinet book starting with the Beginners to the Advanced Book. I lasted about two years and got bored and eventually stopped.

CHAPTER TWO

My First Jazz Band

While still in high school I went to work with my cousin Louie La Rocca who had a fresh egg and poultry route. We would drive to Philadelphia and sell door to door to the colored people. They loved our fresh chicken and eggs. I saved enough money to go back to Spike and get my first wooden clarinet. He recommended this "Buffet" French model. He took my metal clarinet in trade and I paid the difference.

One summer afternoon while I was up in my room practicing, I heard someone call up to me to come down. I looked out my window to see who it was. It was the man who was working next door where they stuffed mattresses. I started to come down and I thought to myself, maybe I was making too much noise and this guy's going to tell me off. He was a big guy with a ruddy complexion and he scared the hell out of me.

He introduced himself as Nick Fazzolari and said I played nice clarinet. I sure was relieved. Then, he went on to say he would always hear me practicing in my room. During our conversation he mentioned he played trombone and was playing with some guys who just got together a little jazz band. He invited me up to their next rehearsal and although I said, "Yes," I was somewhat scared as I never played with a band before.

It was now 1950 and I was about to join my first jazz band. Nick and I talked some more and we had a lot in common. Nick was about eight years older than I and had just recently taken up the valve trombone., He was also originally from Brooklyn.

A few days later Nick took me to meet all the guys in the band. We arrived and I was first introduced to Dom Ippolito who played guitar and was the leader and arranger. Dom was about forty years of age, had been married and divorced, and had this ranch type house where the rehearsals were held. Then, I was introduced to John Mongeluzzo who played cornet; then, Bob Biondi, also guitar; Joe Colucci on drums, and Nick's brother Rocco Fazzolari on tenor sax. They asked me if I was familiar with any Dixieland tunes. I replied, "No," but I would try to play along. They started to play, Basin Street Blues, and I tried playing along thinking I did well when Dom hollered, "Stop!" I found out that I didn't do well and for the rest of the night wrote harmony notes to play.

After that night Nick and i spent a lot of time listening to his jazz records. He had a nice collection including jazz players like Louis Armstrong, Jack Teagarden, Benny Goodman, Bunny Berigan, Bix Beiderbecke and Coleman Hawkins. I couldn't wait to start my own jazz record collection, a little at a time. From all the listening to Nick's records, I was starting to understand the concept and my role as a clarinet player. I would play along with the records and memorized everyone's solos and learned a lot of tunes that way.

The band decided to cut some records at our local radio station for our own personal collection. We recorded, Please Don't Talk About Me, Royal Garden Blues, Basin Street Blues, Nevertheless, Black and Blue; and two original tunes which were written by Dom called, Iona and Red Rag. These recordings are now over 50 years old and occasionally I will play one and realize how bad they really sounded then. Now if I ever get discouraged musically, I put one of these records on and I don't feel so bad.

I was invited back again to play with the band and this time I did much better. They called the band, The Malaga Stompers, named after one of the towns nearby. Except for Nick, I didn't know the guys very well and I was to find out at the next session that they were to play a joke on me. I arrived at Dom's house and I unpacked my horn and the band warmed up with, Muskrat

Ramble. Then I was told Bob Biondi, the second guitar player in the band, was really a hot cornet player. Being a young kid I fell for it and I asked if I could hear him play something. He took John's cornet and started to play all kinds of weird notes and all out of tune. Everyone was looking on like he was the greatest. I was thinking to myself "BOP" sounded great compared to this. Bob asked me real seriously what I thought of his playing! Being young, as well as honest, I said. "I thought you were a better guitar player." When they all heard that they all busted out laughing.

One time the whole band went crabbing near Wildwood, N.J. and I had never been crabbing before. We all met at Nick's house and loaded up the equipment and we were on our way. I had noticed that they also brought along a couple bags of half rotten tomatoes and I asked what they were for. They told me in case any of us got seasick we could suck on the tomato and it would make us feel better. We arrived at the dock and split up into two boats and we each took a bag of tomatoes on board.

After we rowed out a ways and found a good spot for crabbing, the guys in the other boat started to throw these rotten tomatoes at me. The guys in my boat were telling me to cover myself up and at the same time were hitting me in the back of the head with the tomatoes from our boat. Everybody had a good laugh that day but me.

The band took me to hear my first jazz band in Philadelphia. Sidney Bechet on soprano sax, Sidney De Paris on trumpet, Wilbur De Paris on trombone, Teddy Bunn on guitar, Pops Foster on bass, Freddy Moore on drums and Dick Cary on piano and E-flat horn. The band was great and I was in a trance for weeks.

Nick went into the poultry business and had a small store selling live chickens and fresh eggs. By this time I was out of high school. He offered me a job and I went to work for him. I liked the idea because we could talk about music every chance we got. Nick showed me how to kill the chicken by slicing the jugular vein and then letting all the blood drain out through the funnel into a 55 gallon drum while it was kicking itself to death. Then it was put into hot scalding water and the feathers taken off. It was then gutted and cleaned ready for the customer. Business wasn't that good and to make things worse one of Nick's girl friends would hang around the store and Nick would get involved with her and wind up putting out a sign "Closed Today" and they both took off somewhere.

Nick saw a lot of girls and we double-dated a lot with some girls I met through him. These girls were always older than I was and being around Nick they assumed I was older, too. We had some wild times in those days sometimes staying out all night. My mom would ask me the next day where I was and I would say, "Out with Nick." My family liked Nick and knew he was watching out for me and would keep me from getting into trouble.

The band was coming along pretty good now and we took this job playing in this minstrel show being held at the local movie theater. I never played for a large audience before and I was scared. We were introduced and we came out and did a number. When it was my time to solo, I became stage fright. I must have taken six choruses and just could not stop playing. Dom hollered for the band to come in and end it. I was so embarrassed and the band would rib me as being the featured soloist that day.

Dom was starting to arrange for the band. He had this natural talent for it and was self taught. We were only seven pieces but he made us sound like a big band. He would write a different arrangement every week and we became good readers. It was a nice change from playing dixieland. I always liked swing music. By now I was also playing tenor sax and later on took up the soprano.

Jeanne, my older sister, was now married and living upstate in Haverstraw, NY. Her husband Bob was a TV technician and had his own repair shop. I went to visit them one summer and they took me to Bear Mountain and West Point and I thought to myself how nice the scenery was out there. There were small mountains and lots of green to feast your eyes on. Vineland was just the opposite with flat land and poultry farms and fruit orchards.

It was now 1955 and I had just turned 21 years of age. Nick and I must have hit every bar in town to celebrate my manhood.

We talked about the times when I was underage and I couldn't get served and drank soda,. Now I was making up for lost time.

Pop became ill in the Spring of 1955. He had been coughing a lot and was run down from working two jobs. He would work a full day at the power plant and after would do landscaping. He went for a checkup and found out he had tuberculosis. He was sent to Browns Mills Sanatorium for rest and treatment. He was there for a few months and put on weight and was looking good. They told us that the removal of his right lung was necessary and he would be on his way towards a complete recovery. The operation was performed and the following weekend we went to visit him. We found that Pop was very reluctant to have us see him as the operation had left him swollen about the neck and face so that he was unrecognizable.

CHAPTER THREE

All By Myself

He didn't want us to see him like this. We asked how he was feeling and he would not be able to answer above a whisper. They assured us that the swelling would go down and that he would be okay. The very same night just after we had left, Pop passed away. They notified us that he had coughed up something in his sleep and had choked. They asked Mom if they could do an autopsy to see what brought on this choking, but she refused. We will never know what really happened.

The next few days were hectic with the funeral arrangements and everything. My sister Jeanne was a big comfort to Mom as they were close and being the oldest she took care of the arrangements. Pop was only 56 when he passed away.

After awhile Mom decided she wanted to move upstate so she could be near my sister Jeanne who by now had two small children. I decided to stay behind as I had made a lot of musical friends and didn't want to leave the band.

I had this job as a clothing salesman which was okay. All I had to do was find a place for me to live. In the meantime, I got a room at this hotel in town which was a block away from my job. Being on my own was not as easy as I thought it would be with eating at diners every day and accumulating dirty laundry that had to be cleaned and finding every time you wanted to use the hall shower someone was there before you.

Bob Biondi, one of the guitar players in the band who was now playing drums, talked me into moving in with him. It sounded like a good idea at the time and we could share expenses. He told me that he was renting a small house in a field with no one around and we would be able to practice and make all the noise we wanted. I hadn't seen Bob's place yet but took his word for it that it was at least better than living at the hotel. I checked out of the hotel and Bob picked me up to take me to my new home.

When I arrived at his place, which was a couple of miles out of town, I couldn't believe my eyes. There stood this small structure in the middle of a field about the size of a garage. Inside was a couple of cots, a table and chairs, a pot belly stove for heat, and no water. The bathroom was an outhouse in the field. I mustn't forget Bob's set of drums and a cabinet full of jazz records. Now the picture is complete.

I wished I was back at the hotel but I agreed to try it for awhile. It was now winter time and sometimes Bob would forget to get coal for the stove. We would burn paper or wood and anything else that would burn to keep warm. Bob had this old car and each morning it wouldn't start and we had to push it to get it to start. We then would drive to a gas station to use the bathroom so we could wash up. Eventually, Bob got the car fixed.

Bob and Rocky were always debating about what constitutes a jazz beat and where does one put the emphasis—on the first beat or the second beat. It became an obsession with Bob and he was getting hard to live with.

The band was playing a wedding one night and Bob had talked some of the guys to fill their instrument cases with sandwiches and wedding cake. We had enough food to eat all week. I wouldn't recommend it as a steady diet. Bob finally stopped playing with the band as he felt he wasn't playing drums the way he wanted to and it was no longer fun, anymore. He did keep in touch and sometimes would sit in with us for old time's sake. We found a new drummer by the name of George Haines who loved jazz and worked out just fine with the band.

I left Bob's place and found myself a nice apartment a few blocks from town with two big rooms and small kitchen and bath. I had it pretty nice there and the landlady did the house cleaning and gave me clean sheets once a week.

One night I went to sub for this other clarinet player. When I got to the job these guys had to read music and they had this commercial club date style of playing. Nick dropped in to give me moral support.

I got him to sit in and it started to sound better. There was a girl there that night who must have dug the way I played. Every time she gave me the eye I would play my best to make a good impression. She was fairly tall and nice looking. I found out that her name was Dot and she was with another girl named Eva, a pretty little blond.

During intermission Nick and I would talk to them and we got better acquainted as the night went on. We finally talked Dot and Eva into coming to my place for an early breakfast and to listen to some of my jazz records. It was daybreak when we took them home. Dot and I had hit it off pretty good and we spent a lot of nights together. Sometimes I would bring her on my gigs. I really liked her a lot but like all good things it didn't last.

I had quite a good collection of 78 rpm recordings by now and some were collector's items. I had Berigan, the Dorseys, Goodman, Beiderbecke, Armstrong and King Oliver, to name a few.

I found this great record shop in Philadelphia that had everything you would want in jazz records. On Saturday night if I wasn't playing a gig I would take the bus to the city and with all my spare money I would buy records. The owner of the store always greeted me with a big smile and probably thought to himself, "I've got a live one here." Another time when I went back to buy some records I found he no longer was in business and jokingly I thought to myself, "I probably bought so many records that he retired off of me."

While in Philadelphia I would hang out at this club which was on Randstead Street. The name of the club was, The Jam Session, and the owner was a clarinetist who fronted his own quartet there. His name was Billy Krechmer and he was quite well known in the jazz world. He was tired of traveling with bands and wanted to settle in his own place and play the music his way. His trumpet player was Tommy Simms, and Fats Wright on piano, and Steve Davis on bass. I sometimes would talk with him before the gig started as I always got there early. I would hear him practicing doing scales. What a nice tone he had. Once, his advice to me was, "Learn as much as you can about music and develop good technique on your instrument." One time I got the nerve up and asked him if he would teach me clarinet his way. His response was he had a business to run and didn't have time to give clarinet lessons. I often wonder how he may have changed my musical life for the better if he had given me lessons.

One night while in his club in walked Jimmy McPartland and Bud Freeman to sit in with Billy. I realized then this is why his place is called, "The Jam Session." His playing had soul and perfection. Many years later, while living in New York, I looked him up and phoned him. He was 90 years old and living near Atlantic City. He thanked me for remembering him all these years. He had quit the clarinet at age 85. He mentioned that all he was doing was playing a little piano to amuse himself and playing cards with his friends. He sent me a tape of his music and all the bands and musicians he had played with, and some dialogue by him. He passed away soon after at 91 years of age. I am so happy that I got the chance to talk to him before he passed.

Nick had this old Cadillac limousine and we had some good times with it. It looked like something out of the gangster era. One day Nick had to cash a check and parked right in front of the bank. I got out of the car and waited by it until he came out of the bank. I had noticed that the people going by were giving me dirty looks and picked up their pace as if they thought maybe we were robbing the bank. He finally came out and I said to him, "Let's get out of here, I"ll explain later."

We sometimes stopped at this drive-in and ordered a milkshake and a hamburger. If we were dressed up we would make believe we were somebody important and when the waitress left we would have a good laugh over it.

I learned how to drive with this car. One late night Nick was giving me a driving lesson and I almost hit a telephone pole trying to avoid hitting this dog that was crossing the road. Nick chewed me out for that and told me in that kind of a situation it would have been better to kill the dog than get us killed. A few nights later while taking another driving lesson, a similar situation came up as something ran across the road and I just kept going straight ahead and hit it and remembered how it shook the car. I felt I had done the right thing and asked Nick what he thought. He let me have it again saying that I could have avoided that as I wasn't going that fast. I just couldn't win with this guy.

Fred Jackson, who was the antiques dealer in town, got our band its first job at a club called, The College Inn. He knew a couple of guys in the band and loved jazz music. I remember him telling us he was related to the novelist who wrote, "The Lost Weekend" but I don't know if that's true as I never checked it out and we took his word for it. The club was kind of rundown and there were lots of cracks on the wall. We were paid $4.00 dollar a night per man. The money wasn't much but we had a place to play and get some experience and exposure.

George Haines, our drummer, had a cabin in Wildwood, N.J. and in the summer we would go and spend the day with him taking our instruments and having a jam session. George took us to a few clubs in the area and we talked this one owner into letting us play in his place just for fun. He liked us so much that he hired us for six nights a week at twenty dollars a man for the whole summer season. We traveled to the gig each night which was 50 miles round trip.

Philadelphia was a great town to hear jazz and "The Rendezvous" club was the place to hear it. I heard great players there like Louis Armstrong, Jack Teagarden, George Shearing, Louis Prima, and others. We played jobs in Philly for social clubs which were private parties. There was always plenty to drink and eat and our band did plenty of both.

This one gig we played once also had a band playing upstairs for another party and its leader was a tenor sax player named, Mike Pedicin. He was making quite a name for himself at the time. He had a Rock and Roll group which was just being heard then. We found out later most of his crowd came down to hear us and they liked our swing arrangements and they danced and applauded us. I sure felt sorry for that band upstairs.

CHAPTER FOUR

Army Days (Love and Marriage)

This one very cold winter I came down with the flu and I wasn't able to make the weekly rehearsal. The band decided to come up to my apartment to see how I was doing. We never kept the doors locked in those days so the guys walked right in. I was under the covers lying there real still and the way I felt, I wasn't going to move for anybody. They hollered for me and I didn't answer them and they didn't notice me under the covers as I was always pretty thin. I must have blended right into the bed. They figured I wasn't home so they started to play my jazz records. After hearing three choruses of, Jazz Me Blues, I ripped the blankets off of me and shouted for them to stop playing my records as I was sick with the flu. They were shocked as all the time they were there I never said a word They all let me have it after that.

One by one they started in on me. "No wonder he's sick. There's no fresh air in here. All the windows are closed." Then someone else would say, "How could he breath under those covers?" Then they all commented on how skinny I was because they didn't notice me under the covers.

After 7 years with the "South Jersey Saints," which we were now called, I get my draft notice to go into the Army. I was to report on January 7, 1957 to my Selective Service Board in Bridgeton, N.J. From there they sent me to Fort Dix for Basic Training.

While in Basic Training I put in for the Army Band. They made an appointment for me to take the sight reading test. Needless to say I flunked the test. My reading skills were not good enough and I was used to playing swing type arrangements but had no experience reading marching type songs. They were quite difficult for me. I was starting to miss the band and was wondering what was now in store for me. We were told basic training would be for six months before reassigning me.

While at Fort Dix I found out that on Sundays we were able to invite family and friends to our Service Club. One Sunday I invited the band to come up and we put on a concert for everyone there. They all loved it and it was a nice reunion for me. After basic training they sent me to Fort Eustis, Virginia and assigned me to the 88th Transportation Company. I was trained to drive all sizes of vehicles. Once trained, I was shipped to Schweinfurt, Germany.

Before arriving in Germany our ship docked at the Port of Southampton and we were given a 1-day pass to London. If I remember correctly, it was a fairly short train ride, and the train arrived at Charing Cross Station. We immediately took off to see the sites. To some of us that meant young ladies. My friend Howie and I went to Piccadilly Circus and hung out there. Piccadilly Circus was a big square in the heart of London with water fountains and people sitting around having lunch and feeding all the pigeons.

We spotted two girls sitting together and approached them. We found out that they were sisters and one more beautiful than the other. One sister was Valerie and the other Pauline. I somehow was drawn to Pauline but wound up with Valerie. Valerie was blond and beautiful, slim, and 20 years of age. We hit if off very well, I thought, although I think they were taken in by our army uniforms. We all talked over tea and I asked Valerie to write to me in Germany. It became late in the day and we said goodbye as we had to catch the train back to Southampton. Little did I know where fate would take me that day, and that at a future time Valerie would be my future wife and bear my children.

From Southampton we sailed to Bremerhaven in Germany and we were transported to Schweinfurt, our new home for the next 18 months. During the 2nd World War Schweinfurt was completely bombed out because of the ball bearing factories that were there. When I was there in 1957 you would never know there was any desolation a few years prior.

My job while in Germany was to transport troops wherever needed. Mostly we took the infantry to the fields for training purposes. Thank God it was peace time and everyone just played soldier and went through all the simulations of war.

I recall one time while over there they told us there was this Lebanon crisis and they were shipping out the troops right away. We were given orders to drive them to the dock and they would board this ship which would take them to Lebanon.

Someone decided to play this cruel joke on me and they said we also would be going on the ship with our trucks and all. I was scared and beside myself thinking I didn't want to be here in Germany, let alone go to Lebanon. Then we were told we didn't have to go, that someone was having fun with us. Some Fun!

There wasn't much to do for me in Germany to pass the time as we were all homesick and stayed in the barracks a lot writing letters home, etc. Some of us went into town on our weekend pass and we would drink beer and get drunk. I bought a 35-mm camera while over there and took lots of pictures. I also took this course they had on base and learned how to develop my own pictures and enlargements and found it helped to pass the time away.

By now Valerie, the girl I had met in London started to write to me. At first, for awhile, it was one letter a week or so and eventually we wrote almost every day. We exchanged photos of each other, talked about the music we liked and about our lives and families. I was starting to like her very much and she made my time in Germany enjoyable.

I had my clarinet with me and I would practice in the barracks sometimes and other times we would have these little jam sessions for fun. This one guy had a guitar and another had a pair of brushes and kept time. I had a weekend pass and took a train to Frankfurt just to get away from everyone and be on my own. I did not speak German so communication was always hard for me. The music I heard in the beer halls for the most part was polkas and marches— nothing that I had been used to.

By accident I stumbled onto this jazz band in Frankfurt. I had found a room in this hotel upon arriving and then started to walk around the town and to my amazement I heard Dixieland jazz coming out of a second story building. This was the first jazz sounds I heard since leaving the states. I followed the sounds and found myself walking up this one flight of stairs and into this big room with a bandstand and six musicians playing Dixieland. The room had lots of tables and was very crowded. What I noticed first upon entering this place was all these printed cards hanging from strings high overhead with song names on them like, "Jazz Me Blues," "Indiana," "Dixieland One Step," etc. Quite a novel idea I thought. I was enjoying it so much that I stayed until it closed. I came back one more time after that and this time I brought my horn and they let me sit in.

Valerie and I were still writing to each other and I was making arrangements to spend my first month's leave in London so I could spend a lot of time with Valerie. She worked in a department store and I would meet her for lunch everyday and see her at night.

That month we saw a lot of each other and found we were becoming very close. She took me everywhere around London. i got to see all the sites like Buckingham Palace, London Bridge, the Changing of the Guard, Tower of London and the beautiful parks and cathedrals. Every day we went somewhere new and there were dinner, movies, etc.

I recall that Valerie's father was very strict and she had to be in by 10:00 or 11:00 PM. He was also a career army man stationed at the local base called Woolich Arsenal. I met him once before going back to Germany after my leave was up and found him to be this big man who never seemed to smile and very stern looking. My leave was now ending and I didn't want to go back. She saw me off at the train and she waved as I left. I thought how I wish I could stay with her forever. I think I was in love with her but not sure as being away from home and lonely, it just might be infatuation.

We maintained writing to each other and talking about the wonderful times we had together. The following year, just sometime before I was to be shipped home, I was given my last month's leave. Of course, we planned to be together again and enjoy each other. This time around things were getting more serious between us. We talked about me going back home and that we weren't going to see each other any more. I knew in my heart that I was going to miss her and I knew she felt the same about me. One day when she was at work I walked around the town of Woolich and found this jewelry store. I picked out an engagement ring and that night I asked her to marry me. I was scared but she accepted.

I finished my time in Germany and was shipped back to the States to be processed for discharge. Valerie wrote me almost every day and was a great comfort to me. I got discharged in February of 1959 and settled at my Mom's house in Haverstraw, New York where she was now living. I had to find a job to help support myself and music had to be put aside for the moment. There wasn't much work so I applied for this one job to learn how to be an upholsterer and they went out of business. I eventually got a job at a chemical plant.

Valerie came to the States a year later and we were married May 14, 1960. By now I was doing OK at the plant and worked my way up to a foreman's position. We settled in a small apartment and were paying $60.00 a month in rent. I was making about $100.00 a week so I was doing okay. Since I'd been home from the army I hadn't met any jazz musicians to play with. The local newspaper had an ad which read, "Jam Sessions" every Sunday with jazz stars from New York City. The club was called simply, "The Place." I seem to remember that it was on Route 9W in the Haverstraw area. I checked it out one Sunday afternoon and found that some of the players were people like Chuck Wayne Dick Hyman, Bob Wilber and others. The owner's wife had been in show business as a singer and knew a lot of these musicians. She was a heavy set woman with a beautiful voice. I went back quite often hoping to make musical contacts.

One Sunday I met this older woman there by the name of Lynn Delmerico and, to my surprise, she told me she played cornet and had played with all girl bands in the forties in California. I found my first friend that I could discuss music with and found out she loved Dixieland and knew all the tunes. She asked the owner of, "The Place," if we could put together a small group and play for nothing just before the jazz players came in. The owner agreed to try it as he had nothing to lose as it wasn't costing him anything. Lynn got a piano player she knew and I recommended this drummer I had met in the club. His name was Harry Davis and he was a local club date kind of a player, but he liked jazz. We played there a few weeks and I found to my amazement that Lynn could really play that horn. The band was getting better the more we played together and the people seemed to like us. But we didn't have the polish and technique these jazz players had. But we listened and we learned. The owner wasn't getting enough business to support paying the musicians so he closed the place.

I had thought about going into the music business full time but decided against it. Not because I didn't love the music enough, or I wasn't dedicated enough. On the contrary, I loved it just as much if not more than the guy who did it full time. The only difference was I got a paycheck every week and some of these guys didn't. I've worked harder than most as all the years I had a day gig I had to develop my skills in the evening on my time off or take a gig and learn on the job. Music has always been my first love and I have devoted over 50 years towards preserving my kind of jazz music. Just being married a couple of years, now, we were trying for a family but nothing came till a few years later, and did they come, and come, and come.

Anyway, Lynn took me to this club called, "Budges" in Westchester just over the Tappan Zee Bridge to sit in with these two good musicians she had worked with.

The piano player was Gene Hall and he told me he was related to clarinet player brothers Edmond and Herb Hall. The drummer was Herman Bradley who I was told worked with trumpeter "Hot Lips" Page. He was a good swing drummer but he played a little too loud. Herman Bradley was a dark-skinned Negro who was a real nice guy and always had this big smile on his face, on or off the stage. He sure knew how to lead a band and was quite a showman. We became good friends and he liked the way I played and was getting me some work.

On this one job Herman brought this vocalist to sing with the band as I believe it was a holiday weekend and he wanted to give the band a little class. It turned out she sang with the Erskine Hawkins band and sang under the name of Dolly Lyons. She was a pretty, light-skinned Negro with a beautiful voice. Herman had quite a following and through working with him I met a lot of people.

One night he introduced me to this woman by the name of Ginny Avery who played piano. She lived in Port Chester, N.Y. and was the leader of an All-Man Jazz Band, as she called it. She was looking for a clarinet player and asked me if I would want to play. She had this beautiful 200-year old house and once a month on a Sunday afternoon she had this jam session and invited a lot of people to come and hear us.

There was always plenty to eat and drink and everyone had a great time. It was about 1965 when I joined this group and I stayed on and off for about 7 years.

Everyone in this band had other professions: Ed Stanton, trumpet, was a public relations executive; George Bailey, trombone, was in real estate; Joe Licari, clarinet, foreman of a chemical plant; Fred Schombert, tenor sax, worked for the post office; Kim Blanchard, drums, was a water meter executive; Burr Wishart, bass, a Presbyterian minister; and finally Ginny Avery, piano, who taught sewing classes and was a young swinging grandmother.

The band was very active in the Westchester, N.Y., Greenwich, Conn. area. We played concerts and house parties. We even did a half hour spot on the Hugh Downs, "Today Show" on television, coast to coast. His co-host was Barbara Walters. We did the show on Christmas Day in 1966 at 8:00 AM. I remember overhearing Miss Walters say how she thought the music was so loud, and why did they book a band like this so early in the morning? She really hated us. I never cared much for her after that. Being on the show was a good break for us and we got other television offers. The band decided to remain adamantly non-professional. The band was now called, "The King Street Stompers." I first met John Bucher, cornet, and Dick Rath, trombone, subbing in this band.

Dick invited me to sit in with The Smith Street Society jazz band at Kenny's Pub in New York City, which was located on 84th Street east of 3rd Avenue. The leader was Bruce McNichols who played banjo, soprano sax, tin whistle and vocals. He started to hire me for some gigs after that. He must have liked my playing as it's 35 years later and he still hires me. I met and played with good musicians playing in Bruce's band. People like Ed Polcer, Tom Artin, Benny Ventura, Herb Gardner and others.

CHAPTER FIVE

Bob Wilber

I was starting to work with players now that felt the same way about the music as I did. I was getting more concerned about my playing and felt I needed more structure and my tone had a vibrato that I didn't like, and some other concerns that needed correcting.

I heard that Bob Wilber lived in my area and I knew his work and had his Wildcat recordings plus those he made with Sidney Bechet—and some later things he did. I called him up and explained my situation and he set a date for me to come over to his house. At our first meeting he asked me to play something and I remember being nervous. He must have heard something in my playing that made him say, "Okay," and we scheduled some lessons. Usually, that would take place early Saturday afternoons. Occasionally, if he had to work somewhere out of town, he would give me enough work to keep me busy till he got back.

After I was taking lessons for awhile Bob invited me to hear him play at the Riverboat in New York City. The band was great and during intermission Bob introduced me as his student to Bobby Hackett. He was kind of slouched on this sofa he was sitting on and I thought how frail he looked and all he said to me was, "Yeah." He sure could play.

The lessons continued for about a year or so. Bob helped me in more ways than he realizes. At the beginning, I was playing a Buffet clarinet and he got me to switch to a Selmer, Series 9, Star. Bob was playing the same clarinet at that time. My tone sounded much better and much fuller on this clarinet. Bob is totally professional and instills those qualities in his students and makes you want to be a better player. Eventually, he got very busy and the lessons stopped. Every time I play one of his recordings it's like taking another lesson. Bob has been a great influence in my life and I use his playing as the standard for me to try and achieve.

I've kept in touch with Bob all these years, mostly by mail. The last few years Bob has lived in England. If he does a concert in New York I sometimes go see him play. Even today I still ask his advice on musical matters. I just recently recorded a CD with Larry Weiss on piano and we did one of my songs called, "Haunting Melody." I sent Bob a copy and wanted to know what he thought of it. He made some corrections and sent it back to me. His corrections improved the song so much to my liking that I put him down also as composer.

I had forgotten to mention that while I was studying with Bob Wilber in the '60s I composed my first two songs. One was called, "Joe's Lament" and I had brought it to my lesson to show Bob and he started to play it on the piano. He looked up at me and said, "Did you write this?" as if to say it was pretty good for a beginner. I think he liked it but also that he was surprised that the song came out of me.

The other song I wrote was called, "Wilber's Lick." This song is based on a two bar lick that I got from a study book Bob wrote on different jazz licks. I never did write a proper bridge for it and put it aside for a few years. Only recently did I resurrect it and after sending it to Bob to look over I got the ideas and direction to finish it.

About this same period I got interested in oil painting. My old friend Rocco Fazzolari who played sax in my first band, The South Jersey Saints, was a great painter who painted like the Old Masters. He would say, "Anyone can paint and should try it." I tried it for a couple of years and did about 12 paintings until we started to have children. Then, I no longer could find the time to continue.

Only one of the paintings was musical and I called it, "Joe's Jazz Band." Some other jazz artists who painted were Pee Wee Russell, George Wettling and Bob Haggart. That puts me in some great company.

The Metropole was another place to hang out and learn. I got to hear such great players as Red Allen, Zutty Singleton, Cozy Cole, Buster Bailey, Benny Morton, Hank Duncan, Louis Metcalf and many others. This place was always crowded, at least when I was there, mostly on the weekend. When you walked into this place the first thing you noticed on the left was a long bar almost the length of the room. If you managed to find room at the bar, what you found was that the bandstand was above you and you were looking at the feet of the musicians. Across from the musicians there was a large mirrored wall that they could see themselves in while playing. Kind of a weird setup, I thought at the time.

CHAPTER SIX

The Wild One (Thrill of My Life)

This one time that I was there Red Allen was leading the band and Wingy Manone came in and walks by the bandstand making his way to the back so he could get ready for the next set. Red spots him and gets on the mike and announces, "There's Wingy Manone, let's give him a hand." Normally, that's not funny unless you know Wingy had only one hand and wore a prosthetic device covered by a glove.

1970 became a very important year to me as we were blessed with our first child, Theresa, born on December 2nd. The prior years had been fruitless till now and my wife attributes this to finding a good gynecologist and/or about a year before we went to Marian Shrine which is located in West Haverstraw, N.Y. for this special healing service.

The priest gave a special healing mass and afterward Valerie approached this priest who was reputed to have special healing powers and mentioned how we could not have children. He placed his hand on Valerie's stomach and informed her she would have children. Your guess is as good as mine. Was it the gynecologist or the priest, or both, that made the difference? If you were to ask Valerie I'm sure she would say it was a miracle. And it was, as far as I'm concerned.

Another special thing happened to me that year as I got to play with Wild Bill Davison through George Bailey, trombonist with The King Street Stompers. George also played bass and he was playing bass with Wild Bill at the Showboat in Greenwich, Conn. They were thinking of adding a clarinet and George put in a good word for me. When I auditioned for the band Wild Bill didn't have much to say to me. After the gig he took me aside and said, "Look, Kid, if you get to play with the band get yourself a stronger reed and don't end on the same note as me, Always end a third above me."

George was supposed to call me during the week but I didn't hear from him so I figured I blew it. Friday night comes and I get a call from George, "Where are you? You should be down here playing. Bill likes the way you play." You never saw a guy move so fast. I was down there by the second set.

I enjoyed playing with Bill and observing first-hand how he carried on making remarks under his breath about what some pretty girl's under garments looked like or how some were endowed with certain physical attributes. While Bill is looking over at me mumbling some expletive his beautiful wife, Ann, is looking on as if to say, "I know what's going through Bill's thoughts." Ann must have loved Bill a lot to put up with some of the things he is known for, including being a kleptomaniac. Ann had to be a saint.

One night Bill took another gig and sent in a sub by the name of Jack Duffy. It turned out to be that Bill was Jack's mentor and Jack's playing sounded just like Bill Davison. The manager of the Showboat was not aware that a sub was being used. Every time he came by the room he heard what sounded like Wild Bill playing. At he end of the night when it was time to get paid he found out and was very upset over it. The following week we found out that Bill was fired because of that situation.

Having played with Bill was the thrill of my life. i wish it hadn't ended so soon. I could have learned a lot from him. I continued playing after that for awhile but business wasn't as good without a big name like Bill Davison and eventually they got rid of the band.

It was in this band that I first met Red Balaban. Red was playing banjo but also could play bass, tenor guitar and tuba. He started to call me for some gigs. He lead a band at The Town House in Rutherford, N.J. His regular clarinetist was Herb Hall, brother of Edmund Hall, and I would occasionally sub for Herb. Thanks to Red I got to meet and play with very good players.

Some of the people Red had in his bands were Doc Cheatham, Ed Polcer, Paul Riccuci, Bobby Pratt, Marquis Foster, Jackie Williams and Gim Burton. I remember one gig Red put together at a country club in Connecticut. Big Chief Russell Moore, Freddy Moore and myself rode together in Freddy's new car which he recently had acquired. That was some ride! I'm still nauseous just thinking about that trip. Red Richards and Al Hall and Balaban completed the band. I don't remember if there was a trumpet player or not. It was a great band.

Rocky Rockman, owner of "The Old Banjo," in West Haverstraw, N.Y. off Route 9W started a dixieland policy. Rocky loved to sing and was pretty good and he loved the music. Cornetist Dick Roberts, Conrad Janis (trombonist and actor), and myself in the front line. There would be different rhythm sections. It might be Cliff Leeman, Gene Ramey, Alan Cary, Tommy Benford, Barbara Dreiwitz and Howard Johnson. Rocky called the band, "The River Boat Jazz Band." I loved working in this place and it wasn't far from my house. We had a big stage to play on and all the tables had peanuts on them and there was sawdust on the floor. Eventually, Conrad Janis was replaced by Jack Kelly on trombone, not related to Gene Kelly, although there was a strong resemblance. Unfortunately, Rocky went bankrupt. Not because of the music.

Rocky kept the band together and got us a steady gig a couple of towns away in Valley Cottage, N.Y. at a place called, "Kilgallen's." We worked there every Friday and Saturday night. Jack Duffy, Jack Kelly and myself in the front line. The rhythm section, and I have to say the best rhythm section I ever played with, consisted of Cliff Leeman, Gene Ramey and Charlie Nuccio on guitar. I sure enjoyed working in that band and I am sorry we never recorded it. There was a customer who taped us a few times and later I tried to locate him with no results.

Cliff Leeman and I became good friends. He would call me, "His sweet player." His wife, Renée, was a wonderful lady and was always nice o me. They were both great people. Cliff once autographed a picture for me—"To Joe my buddy and a swinger.

Maybe we will have a chance to play sometime without the Plectrom."

Cliff didn't like the banjo very much.

Before I forget, Valerie and I had our second child, John, born on April 30, 1972—to be continued.

After the gig at Kilgallen's came to an end Rocky got the band a job at the "Showboat" in Greenwich, Conn. where I had worked with Wild Bill Davison. Bassist Gene Ramey left the band and moved back to Texas. He was replaced by a female tuba player named Barbara Dreiwitz. She occasionally had subbed before with the band at the "Old Banjo", as well as, "Kilgallen's." She was a pretty lady who, to me, played the tuba the right way. Never aggressive, a nice tone, and a swinging beat.

We have become close friends over the years—along with her husband, Dick, who plays a fine trombone. Even today (2003) we often find we play in the same bands together. Cliff Leeman finally left the band and was replaced with Eric Emory. That was a sad day for me. Cliff was the foundation in the band and now I felt it was going to collapse. Eric turned out to be a decent drummer but not like Cliff. I know that Cliff had very bad eyesight and wore very thick glasses. His wife, Renée, had to drive him to all his gigs. It probably was too far for her to drive each week.

Like the song says, "It's Getting To Be A Habit With Me." You guessed it—our third child, Marian, was born on August 28, 1973. All these interruptions. Now to continue my jazz life . . .

I first met "Big Chief" Russell Moore where I was playing at the "Old Banjo." Sometimes he brought his trombone and sat in. I found out he was a neighbor of mine. He became like a father to me. Russell and his wife, Ida, would invite me and Valerie over to their house quite often. Russell and I would talk about music and all the great players. He would tell me wonderful stories about working with Louis Armstrong and Sidney Bechet. He would show me some home movies he had with Armstrong getting on planes and in hotel rooms and all kinds of stuff.

One of Chief's stories was during WW II he was playing an overseas concert with Louis Armstrong. During the intermission four sailors asked Big Chief why he was playing with all these black guys—expletives surely deleted. Chief replied, "See me after the concert and I'll tell you."

When the sailors came back later Chief beat them to a pulp. He was even put in jail for 24 hours until Louis could post bail for him. There was never a dull moment with Big Chief. He took me to Pow Wows where they would discuss Indian affairs. Once someone asked Russell what tribe I was from and he replied, "The Wop Tribe." Big Chief was a full blooded Pima Indian born on a remote part of the Gila River reservation in Arizona. He is profiled in a wonderful book by Anna Moore Shaw called, "A Pima Pass."

Big Chief was a fine trombonist with his own individual style and sound. If you want to hear some wonderful trombone work listen to the recordings he did with the Sidney Bechet Quartet recorded at Boston's Storyville in the early "50s. Russell and I worked in this band called, "The Galvanized Jazz Band." The leader was a hot cornet player by the name of Fred Vigorito. Chief was the guest star and I would sub the clarinet chair for reed player Noel Kaletsky. It's a wonderful band that's been together many years. This band played at a club called "The Millpond Tavern" in Connecticut.

When Big Chief passed away in 1983 he was 71 years of age. We played a musical farewell to Big Chief at the Nyack Presbyterian Church and at the grave site where he was buried at Oak Hill Cemetery in Nyack, N.Y. We had a nice band for the Chief and those who participated were Ed Polcer, Fred Vigorito, Herb Gardner, Jack Purcell, Buddy Christian and myself.

We did a memorial benefit on January 22, 1984 at Saint Peter's Church with Rev. John Gensel announcing the musical activities. I put a band together to play one of the interludes that day and got Marty Napoleon to play piano who, like the Chief, also worked with Louis Armstrong. Some of the other guests that day who played were, The Galvanized Jazz Band, Dick Wellstood, Jabbo Smith, Major Holley, Freddy Moore, Carol Woods, George Duvivier, Tommy Benford, Dill Jones and Arvell Shaw. Quite an impressive lineup to bid the Chief farewell. I hope he was looking down smiling that day.

Big Chief was a great source of encouragement to me. He used to say, "Look at me, I'm just an Indian off the reservation and I got to work with the great Louis Armstrong."

I feel very fortunate to have had all these musicians in my life to learn from.

About now I was getting a little recognition in the Tri-State area as I played a couple of Pee Wee Stomps and Newport Jazz festivals hosted by the New Jersey Jazz Society. A dear old friend, Pete Balance, for whom I worked for a few times with his band, "The Bourbon Street Paraders," thought it was time to do a profile on me for Jersey Jazz magazine. Pete wrote for the magazine and each month he did a new profile which was called, "Jazz Man of Note."

In this article Pete mentions, and I quote, "After his last gig in New Jersey before leaving for "The Happy Jazz Band" in San Antonio, Texas, Randy Reinhart turned to me and said, "I really enjoyed Joe's playing. He's easy to play with. From the first note of the day he listened to my phrasing and played as if we had been together for years."—end of quote.

This now gives me the opportunity to say what I feel about Randy, and not because of what he said in the article about me. He is the best damn cornet player out there today. I have been saying this for years and you can ask any musician that knows me. They will tell you that when they ask me who do I think is the best player, I always say Randy Reinhart. For years he's had some tough breaks trying to make a name for himself in this crazy business. Only lately has he become in great demand on the festival circuit, and deservedly so.

Fred Vigorito started to use me for other gigs with his band. I believe that Noel Kaletsky hurt his back and was out of commission for quite awhile. Fred kept the band pretty busy. Besides the Millpond Tavern there were concerts and Yale reunions and other things. The one I remember best was when we played at Madison Square Garden. It was a political event on November 1, 1974.

Everyone was there. The governors and ex-governors and the mayor and ex-mayors.

The artists performing were Frank Sinatra, Carol Channing, Alan King, Ben Vereen, Melba Moore and our band playing during the intermissions. We got to hang out in this large guest room with plenty of food and drink for everyone. Sinatra had his own guest room, of course, and I must have counted at least five large body guards surrounding him at all times. Alan King hung out with us in the guest room and I remember him kidding all of us that we looked too young to be drinking. He seemed to be a nice man.

CHAPTER SEVEN

The Dixieland Bands (Jazz Clubs)

Before I go on I must mention that another bundle from heaven had arrived in the form of a baby boy named Dominic who was born on December 31, 1974. Hope you are keeping track as it's far from over.

In this same year, just a few months earlier, I lost a dear friend and mentor, Dom Ippolito who was the band leader in my very first band. He was just 69 years of age and much too young.

On May 16, 1975 I finally got to hear and meet Benny Goodman, my hero, and the reason I play clarinet today. The local newspaper said, "Goodman Sextet to wail at Nanuet Star Theatre." That was good enough for me. His band consisted of Hank Jones, piano; Urbie Green, trombone; Ronnie Bedford, drums; Bucky Pizzarelli, guitar; Zoot Sims, tenor; Mel Davis, trumpet; and Slam Stewart, bass.

The band was great and after the concert I sheepishly hung around till the crowd thinned out. I waited my chance and saw Benny was not engaged in anything and cautiously approached him. I was nervous. I said something like, "Hi, Benny, I play clarinet too and enjoyed your playing very much." He mumbled something back and I took off.

In 1976 I joined a band called, The Speakeasy Jazz Babies. This band was quite active at the time. The leader was John Bucher, a fine player, who has played consistently well all the years I've known him. Also in the band was Dick Dreiwitz on trombone, Dick Miller on piano, Richie Barron on drums, Barbara Dreiwitz on tuba. The guitar chair started with Mike Peters, then Carmen Mastren and, after he passed away, Marty Grosz joined the band.

The Red Blazer, Too restaurant started a jazz policy and hired the band. We also brought in Betty Comora to sing with the band. Dennis Carey was the owner and we were his steady Friday night band. We lasted there over five years and then Dennis wanted to move us to another night and the band objected. He wanted to give us a slower night hoping we could build it up. We decided not to do it and the band left.

I must say that Dennis Carey loved the music and all these years he has maintained three different jazz clubs. The first being on Third Avenue on the East side and then, a few years later, opened a place on 46th Street in the theater district and, finally, his last club was on West 37th Street called, The Hideaway.

I worked there for awhile with the Stan Rubin, Tigertown Five. Leading the band was Herb Gardner on piano and trombone. It was a nice little band but only drew a sparse audience. He tried everything, even a Cabaret Night, but could not get a good following. Personally, I think it closed because nobody could ever find this place. The "Hideaway" was an appropriate name for the place. He kept a lot of musicians working over the years and as of this writing is trying to find another spot where the rents are not too high. That's very hard to do in New York City.

The Speakeasy Jazz Babies had a decent following and we were invited to play jazz festivals and stomps, jazz societies and concerts. We loved having Carmen Mastren in the band. He was the sweetest man, always smiling, and didn't have a mean bone in his body. I was thrilled playing with Carmen and knowing that he was that wonderful guitarist playing on those 1945 recodings with Sidney Bechet and Muggsy Spanier. He would always say to me that he thought I sounded like Jimmy Dorsey in my upper clarinet register. We recorded two albums with this band. One with Carmen Mastren and later on with Marty Grosz, a great rhythm guitarist, entertainer and friend.

May I please interrupt for a moment to say Valerie just gave birth to twin boys named David and Francis, born March 1, 1976. Now I shall continue if my wife doesn't bother me with anything.

The Speakeasy Jazz Babies had a double identity working as THE New Orleans Funeral and Ragtime Orchestra at Michael's Pub every Monday night backing movie maker Woody Allen who played New Orleans style clarinet. I would get to sub for Woody when he was out of town. In those days Woody made all his movies out of town, which was good for me. Then, later, Woody made all his movies in New York, which was bad for me. I actually met him once. We were introduced and we shook hands and he never looked at me. He was a very shy and introverted individual.

Eventually, I got fired as the owner Gil Weist didn't want me to work there anymore. When I asked a band member why I was fired I was told I looked too Italian. Other players got fired for reasons like . . . he's too tall, too short, has a beard, whatever. If Gil knew Woody was not playing that night, whoever the sub was would be escorted to a back room not to be seen by the customers until it was time to play. Surprise! "No Woody." Although it was the best gig in town, it was very embarrassing for the clarinet players. At least it was for me.

About this time we were asked to play this big benefit for Rudy Powell at Storyville on East 58th Street. Besides our band, the other bands were Louis Metcalf's, Pioneers of Jazz; Clyde Bernhardt and The Harlem Blues and Jazz Band; Brooks Kerr Trio; and the Sol Yaged Combo. The benefit was coined, "The Friendly Fifty All-Stars." The company we kept that day was unbelievable with such stars as Herman Autrey, Eddie Barefield, Tommy Benford, Happy Caldwell, Al Casey, Sonny Greer, Benny Morton, Joe Thomas, Andy Kirk . . . and the stars went on and on. Then I think to myself what the hell was I doing there among Jazz History.

Around March of 1978 Ed Polcer started to call me for gigs at the new Eddie Condon Club on West 54th Street that Red Balaban opened up next to Jimmy Ryan's. Herb Hall was the clarinetist in the band and later when Herb went back to Texas Bobby Gordon replaced him. I learned a lot playing in this band as everyone was a World Class player. Ed would call me to sub for Saturday and

Tuesday nights. Tuesday nights were special at Condon's. They had two bands alternating and on the last set of the night both bands played together, ending a wonderful night of jazz. I got to work with John Bunch, Jimmy Andrews, Connie Kay, Bob Haggart, Vic Dickenson, Pee Wee Erwin and Dill Jones.

The first time I played with John Bunch while at Condon's he came over to me during an intermission and he said, "You like Benny Goodman, don't you? I can hear it in your playing." I replied that I liked Benny very much when he played with Ben Pollack. Goodman was a hot player then.

Bobby Gordon went back to California and if my memory serves me correctly Polcer hinted to me if I might be interested in the clarinet spot. As much as I wanted to, I couldn't. I had a day gig paying some bills and was raising a young family. To survive I needed the music as well. It was hard on my family working all day and coming home to rush off to some gig. My wife has put up with this all these years and knew from the very beginning that music always came first with me, as that's who I am.

Clarinetist Jack Maheu replaced Bobby Gordon and stayed till the place closed. Although I was playing with all these jazz stars I was always a bit nervous and felt intimidated at times. I would think, "Maybe I'm not good enough." All my musical life I have never taken a compliment very well. Maybe that was my problem, and I should try to think more positive about my playing.

Well, anyway, a building project came in and tore Condon's down, as well as, Jimmy Ryan's—the last jazz landmark. Some one needed to build another hotel or skyscraper, like we didn't have enough already. That's progress for you.

Speaking of progress, we just had another child, a baby girl named Ann in the year 1978. I think by now you know we are practicing Catholics.

I was getting a lot of work this year picking up new gigs besides the local stuff. Bill Lezotte, a very good guitarist, started giving me gigs out in Connecticut. We worked a steady gig at a club called, Mackenzie's By The Sea, in Stanford. The band was called, Basin Street Four. Myself on clarinet, Fred Vigorito on cornet, Art Hovey on bass and Bill Lezotte on guitar. We kind of fashioned the band on the Muggsy Spanier/Sidney Bechet Hot Four. Also, we worked another club called, The Royal Footman in Hamden, Connecticut. We also put a group together playing the music of Benny Goodman and we called it, "Swing 39." We would add vibes and drums.

One day Bill Lezotte called me to confirm this gig we had for a country club and mentioned he was having trouble getting a cornet player.

I told Bill, "Listen, I have an idea. Let me call Kenny Davern and ask him if he would play lead on his soprano sax." I called Kenny and he thought it was a good idea and accepted the gig

What a band it was that day! Kenny played a beautiful lead and we didn't miss having a cornet player at all. Also in the band that day were Porky Cohen on trombone, myself on clarinet, Fred Giordano on piano, Pete Compo on bass, Joe Madding on drums and Bill Lezotte on guitar.

Years later Kenny asked me to play in his place at the Cornerstone in Metuchen, New Jersey with his band. Kenny was doing the sound-track for a Woody Allen movie that day. That night I worked with John Bunch, Tony De Nicola and Bill Holaday. I was very flattered that Davern asked me, as he could have gotten anybody.

1979 brought the Licaris another baby boy, and named him Joseph, Jr. My God, will this ever end?

I call this the year of the Joe's as the Speakeasy Jazz Babies got this gig to open a new store in Fairfield, New Jersey. They billed us as direct from Michael's Pub, one of the world's greatest Dixieland bands. I think maybe a slight exaggeration, don't you agree, but what the hell.

This was not a typical opening. This place was huge with door prizes, buffet luncheon and open bar. The guest that day signing autographs was none other than world-famous sports celebrity, Joe Di Maggio. I noticed that he was nicely dressed and that he was a very handsome man. He would be signing autographs while we were playing music.

We decided we would play for him, "Take Me Out To The Ball Game." After we were done he turned around and gave the band a big smile. I guess he approved and it brought back memories for him. We heard he was paid $10,000.00 for his appearance that day. I got paid $80.00 for playing four hours. I think I'm in the wrong business.

Soon after that the band played a Jewish benefit for the J.C.C. on the Palisades. This time we were billed as, "Woody Allen's Favorite Dixieland Jazz Band, The Speakeasy Jazz Babies." Also there was star-maker Pete Bennett plus TV and Radio Personality, Joe Franklin. During the course of the evening they fed us and Joe Franklin was seated across from us. I expected him to talk his head off like he does on his radio show. He sat there and never said a word to any of us.

John Bucher was a stock broker on Wall Street and he got us a gig to play for The Wall Street Olympic Athletic Committee. Bruce Hopewell, a jazz concert producer, got all the musicians together for the different venues and times to perform. The first band was lead by Machito with his 11-piece band. Then they had, "The Wall Street Olympic Jazz All-Stars"—and all-stars they were. The players were Ellis Larkins, Roy Haines, Howard McGhee, Tommy Flanagan, Connie Kay, and we were the Dixieland Band.

In 1980 I went to Aruba with vocalist Natalie Lamb and her New Orleans Hot Six featuring Dill Jones on piano. The rest of the band was made up of the following: Mike Slack, trumpet; myself on reeds; Bruce Payne, trombone; Barbara Dreiwitz, tuba; and finally, Mike Burgevin on drums.

We stayed at the beautiful Aruba Beach Hotel. We played a concert in the hotel every night and at the end of our stay in Aruba we played a concert for all the natives, as well as tourists, in their big concert hall. We did the very first Jazz Festival Aruba ever had. Aruba is known as The Little Dutch Isle in the Netherlands Antilles. The island is very small, about two to three miles in any direction. The band played at night and saw the sights during the day.

Aruba was a beautiful place to be and I would recommend it to everyone. The weather was perfect, at least when I was there in late September. The sand was clean and the water was clear and green. I hung out mostly with Dill Jones and his wife Wendy and Barbara Dreiwitz and her husband, Dick. Mike Slack was off by himself seeing the island on a motor bike. Bruce Payne and Natalie Lamb were off somewhere doing their thing. Mike Burgevin, who is an accomplished painter, was off with his easel painting the local scenery.

It almost seems like we were avoiding each other but we saw each other at breakfast everyday and, of course, when we played in the band together. Dill and I went swimming almost every day and then a few of us would go into the village and find a cold beer.

One had to be very careful being in the sun too long as we were very close to the Equator. They recommended no more than 15 minutes or you could badly burn. We mostly would stay under a shaded palm-like tree or they had these Cabanas with tin roofs that you could get under. Just before coming home most of us went on this large sailing ship and I forgot to bring a shirt to cover myself, as you don't know you are burning. You feel the splash of water from the waves and cool breezes and think every thing is fine. I looked like a lobster when I got home and could do nothing for over a week.

We never got back there as we hoped they would do a jazz festival again the following year, but nothing happened. I understand now that they have jazz festivals there but the music is Modern jazz.

At this time I was playing at The Red Blazer Too on Friday nights and David Ostwald a tuba player, and later also on bass sax, had a band playing on Sunday nights at the Red Blazer. Recently, talking to David he reminded me that after our band quit, his band, The Blazer Bobcats, had replaced us on Friday nights—which I didn't remember.

Anyway, David approached me one day and asked to play in a new band he was starting and he called it, The Gully Low Jazz Band. I remember we took these publicity pictures of the new band as we were scheduled to begin a series of concerts, the first being at the Marriott in Arlington, VA for the Potomac River Jazz

Club. We also did a concert for the Delaware River Jazz Society in Gibbstown, NJ.

This band leaned heavily on Bix's, Wolverines and Louis's, Hot Five and Seven. In fact, it was Armstrong's seldom heard tune, "Gully Low Blues," that provided the name for the band. In the band were Randy Reinhart, cornet; myself on clarinet, Joel Helleny on trombone, "Deacon Jim" Lawyer, banjo and vocals; David Ostwald, tuba and Leader; and, finally, Fred Stoll on drums. I enjoyed playing with this band especially since Randy was in the band. He has always been my favorite cornet player.

This was a good band and I enjoyed playing with them. When we did the concert for the Delaware Jazz Society, the first band I ever played with, The South Jersey Saints, surprised me by attending the concert and afterwards we reminisced about old times. It was nice to see my old band members and to see how we had all grown older and still have a love for this music.

On one of Dave's gigs, I am not exactly sure when it was, I first met George Avakian. It had to be after 1991 as that's when Dave first met him. What a legend this guy is in the recording business. Dave became friendly with him and he came to one of Dave's gigs. He was very nice to me, I recall, and seemed to me to be a very nice man.

He must have been impressed with my playing that day and was very complimentary. He told me that he had not known about me and if he had known about me years ago he would have recorded me. I think coming from him that 's about the best compliment one can get. He has produced so many jazz artists on recordings and has won numerous awards, and deservedly so.

I remember David Ostwald used to come in to the Red Blazer every Friday to listen to The Speakeasy Jazz Babies and he would bring his tape recorder and then go home to practice and learn the tunes. Dave had just arrived from Chicago where he went to college and was now living in New York. One night he came in with his tuba and John Bucher let him sit in. Dave said he thought he had died and went to heaven.

Dave and I were recently talking on the phone about different things and he reminded me of an incident I completely forgot about. It seems one Friday night I had arrived late as my daughter Ann had been born earlier that day. When the band saw me coming in they broke into, "I Got Rhythm."

Dave has maintained his band for quite a few years and although the personnel may change from time to time he uses only top players. When I have been asked to play with Dave's band in the past I got to work with players like Randy Sandke, Howard Alden, Arnie Kinsella, Frank Vignola and Ed Polcer. It doesn't get much better than that.

A few months after we got back from Aruba with Natalie Lamb's, Hot Six sometime in 1981, Natalie had a string of gigs for us. The one that stands out the most was this one gig on The Binghamton Ferry Restaurant which is permanently docked in Edgewater, New Jersey on the Hudson River overlooking New York City. We had to play a special show which required a special piano player. In walks this black piano player and I had no idea who he was. Natalie introduced me and said, "Meet Sammy Price."

I knew he was a famous Blues and Boogie Woogie piano player. He has recorded with Jimmy Rushing and Sidney Bechet and has played with a lot of bands. He turned out to be a wonderful player and I was glad I had the opportunity to play with him thanks to Natalie.

I don't see Natalie too much these days. The last I worked for her was three years ago. She mainly just works with a piano player. I guess it gets less complicated that way and easier to get work.

This same year brought some sadness and some joy as my good friends Carmen Mastren and Pee Wee Erwin passed away. Carmen was our guitarist at The Red Blazer and I worked with Pee Wee a couple of times at Eddie Condon's.

The joy was my son, Michael, who was born on August 21, 1981. Be patient, it's almost over . . . and you won't need to keep counting any longer.

The next couple of years had me working in four new groups which were Warren Vaché and the Syncopatin' Six; Johnny Blowers, Giants of Jazz; The Dill Jones Trio; and, finally, The Bernie Privin Quartet.

The way I got to play with Warren Vaché was that his regular clarinetist Nick Sassone got sick. I don't remember what it was but he couldn't play for quite a while. Warren called me to replace Nick. We worked a few places like Jack O'Connor's on Route 22 in New Jersey and the Cornerstone Restaurant in Metuchen, New Jersey.

Warren had some wonderful players in his bands. Usually, he had Chris Griffin on trumpet, Benny Long on trombone, Jimmy Andrews on piano, Johnny Blowers on drums and himself on bass. Sometimes, Warren Vaché, Jr. replaced Chris Griffin. I kid everyone and say that I got to play with Benny Goodman's trumpet section as I also worked with Bernie Privin and Jimmy Maxwell who sometimes subbed at The Red Blazer for John Bucher. These trumpet players I mentioned all worked for Benny Goodman in the early '40s.

CHAPTER EIGHT

The Band Leaders (Small Groups)

Sometime in 1982 Bob Benitz and Nancy Hutka from the Cornerstone began traditional jazz in their place and Warren Vaché, Sr. and His Syncopatin' Six was the House Band. Warren had to supply music and musicians four nights a week. They had music on Wednesday, Friday, Saturday and on Sunday. He kept a lot of musicians working with that kind of schedule. He did have a big pool of players to pick from. The clarinet players, besides myself, were Clarence Hutchenrider, Kenny Davern, Russ Whitman, Nick Sassone, Artie Baker and others. I don't remember how long that went on but many years later it continues to the present (2003).

At one point, a bass player named Bill Holaday took over and hired just quartets with himself usually playing bass. This one time, Kenny Davern sent me in to take his place and Bill Holaday was the bass player. We had never worked together before that. Later, during the gig, Bill said he liked my playing and would call me again. At this writing, I am still waiting. I found out just recently that he passed away.

Something About Reviewers . . . I always liked John S. Wilson the best. John worked for the New York Times. Out of all the reviewers, he was always fair and never wrote anything bad about anyone. He did a nice piece on our band playing at The Red Blazer.

The article read, "John Bucher Group is Fixture at Red Blazer." On this occasion John said, "My playing was joyful with a bubbling bounce." Some other samplings of what has been said about me are: "Skillful playing", "Warm lower register mumblings", "Licari's fluid clarinet", "Provides competent counter-part", and—this is my favorite—"Joe Licari, while not a virtuoso clarinetist, gets in some good licks now and then."—"Joe Licari, a fine clarinetist, who deserves wider recognition."

These are just a few things written about me. You wonder what they are listening to, sometimes, as they are all so different. I try not to worry about that sort of thing anymore. I know if I'm playing good or not.

I guess I first met Johnny Blowers in Warren Vaché's band. I liked working with him. He was a very good drummer. He had played in Bunny Berigan's band in 1938 and later on with Bobby Hackett, Eddie Condon, Yank Lawson and studio work in the 1960s. He had very good time in his playing which was important to me. He had his own band then and called it Johnny Blowers', "Giants of Jazz."

The "Giants of Jazz" played a couple of different places. One being The Cornerstone Restaurant and the other O'Connor's Beef and Ale House in Watchung, New Jersey. I recall one great band Blowers put together for a gig at the Cornerstone. I have it on tape and it sounds wonderful but the balance may be slightly off to possibly make a CD out of it. Randy Reinhart is on cornet and sounds just marvelous. Also, Tom Artin on trombone swinging out and myself on clarinet. The rhythm section consisted of Johnny Blowers, drums; Jane Jarvis, piano; and Warren Vaché, Sr. on bass. Jane Jarvis was great and that was the first time I had played with her. I did work again with her later on.

Blowers also had this great steady gig at O'Connor's. They advertised it as, "O'Connor's Presents Jazz featuring Johnny Blowers' "Giants of Jazz." The only thing was that they were only Quartets. The different rhythm sections would change each week when I might be playing with Don Coates, John Halsey, Bob Smith and Dill Jones on piano. On bass it might be Bill Crow or Warren Vaché.

This was very good practice for me as I had to play lead. I learned many melodies that way and I enjoyed the interplay between the players—although Johnny Blowers usually directed traffic.

Right here will be my last notation on the subject of having children. My last child, a baby boy named Paul, was born to us on June 21, 1984. Now that this is recorded I can go on with this book without further interruptions. My prayers were finally answered. Now all I have to do is figure out how to support all those kids.

Working with Bernie Privin (trumpet) was a pure delight. He was a gentleman in every way but had this devilish funny side in him at little things he would come out with. If I would say to him, "Did I sound okay on that solo?" He would reply with something like, "I'll be the judge of that." He was fun to be around.

I first met him on a gig and I don't remember what band it was but Dick Dreiwitz and I and Bernie went up in the same car. He would have us in stitches—a real nice man. We exchanged phone numbers and he started to call me for his band. Most of his jobs were in Westchester. I believe he lived in Hartsdale at the time in a high rise apartment, as I remember meeting him there once.

At the time I played with him his lip was not in the best of shape as he was having a little difficulty getting out the notes. He would play the ensemble with me then he would rest his lip leaving me alone to play on my own. He hardly took solos and left that to me.

Sometimes he had a six-piece band but most times just a Quartet with Bernie and myself in the front line plus piano and drums. I remember he used a Doctor Bob Litwak on drums and I don't remember the piano player's name. He used Bucky Calabrese on bass in the bigger group. I heard that eventually Bernie went to Jimmy Maxwell for help with his lip. Maxwell was a great teacher and had specific exercises for lip problems. I think eventually Bernie just stopped playing.

I would save some of Bernie's correspondence as his letters always had a humorous ending. For instance, this is a letter I got from him, "Dear Joe, Yes I did get your card from Aruba and thank you very much. In answer to your questions: The organist was Sy Mann now residing in Florida, and the guitarist was Don Arnone. Hope all is well with you, and the best of reeds in '81."

Another letter he wrote me went like this, "Dear Joe, Enclosed is the Django Reinhardt album we made in Paris in 1944 with Mel Powell, Ray McKinley, Peanuts Hucko and Joe Shulman, with some room left on the cassette. I have included a side I made during a concert in Sweden with Ovie Lind's Quintet which featured a gal who imitated Billie Holiday—followed by a side I made with Charlie Parker in which I had 8 bars. And to close it out I included, "I've Got A Crush On You," which I recorded with Al Caiola in 1955."

Up your Happy New Year.

One time he sent me a tape of him playing with Wild Bill Davis the jazz organ player. I noticed on one of the numbers he sang, "Thanks A Million," and I remarked, "I didn't know you sang."

He replied, "Why not, I paid for the Session."

Continuing with funny correspondences, I found one here from Jimmy Maxwell, great trumpet player, who replaced Harry James in Benny Goodman's band. I started to work with Jimmy in the Jazz Babies at the Red Blazer subbing for John Bucher. After not seeing him for awhile he wrote me this note:

> "Hi Joe,
>
> I hope we'll get together soon. It's been July since I last had the pleasure of hearing your sweet tones. If I don't hear you soon I may have to listen to Sol Yaged!! In the meantime, you are still the greatest!!—JIM

As I mentioned before, I went to Aruba with Dill Jones. But I had met Dill long before that. Dill was our first call sub at the Red Blazer on Third Avenue when Dick Miller took off. Dill was the finest player I ever played with—maybe next to Dick Wellstood, who also was one of a kind.

Dill's technique was impeccable. He could feel at home playing Scarlatti pieces or Ragtime and Dixieland standards or just a pretty ballad. He was a sweet man who loved to talk and always had a smile on his face. He also liked a good drink which sometimes he would over indulge in. But it never affected his playing.

Dill used me occasionally in a working Trio he had with Pete
Compo, a wonderful bass player in the Slam Stewart tradition. I
remember playing a wedding with the trio and I believe it was a
friend of Dill's who was giving the reception. I recorded us that
day and the band sounded pretty good although we were playing
outside and it was starting to get noisy.

Just recently I rediscovered the tape and I found a Blues on it
that we did based on, Tin Roof Blues. I took about three choruses
on it never playing the melody but invented my own tune. I like
it so much that I had my friend, Dan Fox, who is a guitarist, a
music writer and a transcriber, take it and transcribe the music
from the tape for me. Dill is no longer with us as he passed away
with cancer in 1984. In his honor, I call the piece, "Blues For
Dill."

In the last six months of his life I watched Dill go down hill.
He had throat cancer and they had to operate and he was given a
voice box to communicate with. It was so sad to have to hear him
through this voice box amplified. The last time I got to play with
him was at O'Connor's on New Year's Eve of 1983. At that point
he had stopped eating and he looked terrible. He played brilliantly
to the very end. That's just the way he wanted it. He died on June
22, 1984.

There is a wonderful little book on the Discography of Dill
Jones compiled by David Griffiths that came out in 1996. This
book is available from Gerard Bielderman, Leie 18, 8032 AG,
Zwolle, Netherlands. Phone: 038 4537821.

From the mid-60s to the mid-80s there existed, at least that
I'm aware of, a jazz society that was called, The Connecticut
Traditional Jazz Club, Inc. and Pete Campbell hosted the concerts.
Unlike other jazz societies they would invite a different jazz band
to perform every other month.

Their concerts would be recorded and at the end of the year
they would represent the different bands by putting two or three
of their best songs on an album. Then, they would send the leader
a copy and the following year they were offered for sale to all the

members. This was repeated each year with a new album to represent the year before.

I always thought that this was a great idea and had hoped other jazz societies would have adopted a similar practice. I know that I am represented at least five times over those years playing with different bands. I wish it still existed as they were good to play for and a lot of us musicians miss that. I believe it was 1985 that they stopped recording the musicians as maybe it was no longer profitable to do so.

The last time I worked for them was with vocalist Betty Comora in April of 1985. The Jazz Club asked Betty to put a band together for an upcoming concert, and a good band it was. It was advertised as "Betty Comora and Her All-Star Jazz Band." The rest of the players were Randy Sandke, cornet; Dan Barrett, trombone; Bucky Calabrese, bass; John Halsey, piano; and Chuck Speis on drums. We never got recorded so I'll never know how we sounded that day.

Another jazz society I enjoyed playing for was The Long Island Traditional Jazz Society. The Speakeasy Jazz Babies did a concert every year for them. It was held at The Knights of Columbus Hall in Babylon, New York. We always had an enthusiastic crowd and they were mostly older people who attended. We were recorded on December 8, 1990 and we produced a nice cassette for sale. In the band were John Bucher, Joe Licari, Dick Dreiwitz, Dick Miller, Marty Grosz, Barbara Dreiwitz, Fred Stoll and vocalist Barbara Lea. We kept coming back every year and each year the crowd got thinner. We found that they were dying off on us and, eventually, I guess we killed most of them as they stopped having concerts. This sounds like a joke but it's kind of sad when you think about it.

Between 1984 and 1989 I worked with drummer Chuck Slate's Trio. Chuck was very popular in the New Jersey area. He kept me busy working three gigs a week with his band alone. Keep in mind that I still maintained different day gigs to support my family, which I had to do to survive. There was a lot of jazz being played in New Jersey at that time and you had Chuck Slate to thank for that.

He believed in the music and kept it going. Over the course of those years we played a lot of gigs and the piano players changed a lot. When I first started playing with Chuck the piano player was Charlie Queener, quite an accomplished musician who loved Stravinsky and composed many classical pieces of his own which have been played by symphony orchestras.

Charlie also worked with clarinetist Joe Marsala on 52nd Street in New York City. After awhile Hank Ross played for quite a long while. Hank has been one of my favorite players through the years and is more suited to my kind of playing. Other subs have been Joe Acito and Fred Fischer.

Chuck's Traditional Jazz Band was usually a six-piece band and we would add the extra pieces to play the local festivals like, The Pennsylvania Jazz Society, The Pee Wee Stomps, JVC Jazz Festival and the New Jersey Jazz Society. Chuck Slate has been a dominant figure in the Central Jersey jazz scene for many years, and has promoted many of the new jazz stars that we have playing today.

The years that I worked with Chuck we maintained steady gigs at The Bernardsville Inn and The Store in Basking Ridge, N.J; and Rod's and the Ride and Hunt Club also in Bernardsville, N.J. Many people may not know that Chuck is one of the original founders of the New Jersey Jazz Society. He is not always given credit for it.

Playing with Chuck brought us many write-ups in the local papers. On March 21, 1985 The Bernardsville News did a big article on Chuck and devoted a nice section to me which said the following:

"Joe Licari's musical career started when he joined The South Jersey Saints at age 16. After a stint in the army between 1957 and 1959 Licari became a familiar figure in most of the prominent New York jazz rooms. Among the jazz greats he has worked with are Big Chief Moore, Wild Bill Davison, and Bob Wilber (with whom he studied clarinet in the mid-60s). At the moment he is one of the few jazz clarinetists, along with Wilber, Kenny Davern and Phil Bodner—who are keeping the clarinet before the public"

The last few years Chuck's playing has been limited as he developed carpal tunnel syndrome. Nowadays, I may play an occasional gig with Chuck but still have maintained our friendship over the years.

Just recently I came across a tape of a recording we did at the Watchung View Inn in Bridgewater, N.J. I had forgotten about it and I started to play it. It was just a Trio with the wonderful and inventive playing of pianist Jimmy Andrews who I worked with years before at Condon's. I liked what I heard and called Chuck to see if he was interested in making a CD out of it. Chuck wasn't interested and said, "Do what you want with it," as it was okay with him.

The piano on this recording was slightly out of tune but with Jimmy playing it you quickly forgot about it. Anyway, I produced it and at the same time formed Claril Productions. It came out in 2000 but originally was recorded in 1984. Marty Grosz was kind enough to do the liner notes for me. I called it, "That's A-Plenty" and had 9 other tunes on it.

I also did another CD on my label, with Larry Weiss on piano, in a studio which I had mentioned earlier and that had 18 tunes on it. It is called, "Haunting Melody" after an original tune I wrote with some assist from Bob Wilber.

I remember getting a call from Warren Vaché, Sr. for a gig at Jack O'Connor's on Route 22 in Bridgewater, N.J. and he told me that Doc Cheatham was playing trumpet. I already had a gig for that day but mentioned to hold off as I would get a sub for the other gig. Lucky for me I got one and accepted Warren's gig. I'm so happy that I did as Doc was a delight to play with and I only worked with him maybe once before. This man, who was over 80 years at this time and 30 years my senior, was playing really well with a lot of energy.

I also have some great pictures with Doc and I playing together. During intermissions we get to eat and I saw Doc sitting by himself and I joined him. He mentioned to me he thought I played nicely and I thanked him for that.

His nickname, "Doc" came about from having a lot of relatives in the medical profession. A very accomplished musician who worked with everybody and I'm glad I got the chance to work with him. Also in the band that day were Ernie Hackett on drums, Don Coates on piano and Warren on bass and myself on reeds.

On Sunday, September 14, 1986, The New Jersey Jazz Society put on the super jam session of the year. It was a giant tribute for the late and dear friend of mine, Cliff Leeman. The tribute in his memory was held at a large facility called Farcher's Grove in Union, N.J. I was scheduled to play that day along with many others too numerous to mention. Some of the finest jazz musicians were there that day to play for Cliff—master of the drums and a great jazzman. The music was so wonderful that day.

What they did, as there were so many musicians, was to put different guys together to form a band depending on who was there at the time. I arrived and was informed that I would be going on for the next set. When I approached the stage to play, the other musicians who were to join me were Herb Gardner on trombone, Bill Crow on bass, Phil Napoleon on piano and the great Joe Morello on drums. I had never played with Joe and found him to be just marvelous. I thought, "This is going to be a great band," and it was.

For whatever reason, Joe Morello played three numbers with us and he had to leave. He was replaced by Don Robertson. Vocalist Betty Comora sang a few numbers with the band. After the set was over I went to pay my respects to Renée, Cliff's wife, and we chatted for a bit. I had purchased one of Cliff's albums that were for sale there and I asked Renée to write something on the album in Cliff's honor. This is what she wrote: "To Cliff's sweet player—you know how much he loved you—and I do, too." . . . Renée

For part of 1986 and 1987 I got to work on Tuesday nights with the Washboard Kings at the Cajun Restaurant in New York City. Stan King was the leader and played washboard. Barbara and Dick Dreiwitz were in the band at that time and recommended me. I don't remember which clarinet player I replaced. It might have been Orange Kellin, but I am not sure. Also in the band were

Eddy Davis, Peter Ecklund, Lew Macallif and Paul Bacon. This was a fun band to play with and I remember that musicians liked sitting in with this band. Then, later on, they decided to change the band personnel by replacing Barbara and Dick Dreiwitz. I quit soon after that.

Sometime after that Michael Velasco started hosting jazz nights at The Wall Street Café in Lyndhurst, N.J. He was hiring a lot of different jazz bands to play there every week. I worked there with a couple of different bands and Mike asked me to bring in a group. I booked Marty Grosz on guitar, Greg Cohen on bass and Jimmy Maxwell on trumpet. I called the group, "Joe Licari's Big Four." It was a great band. I thought I couldn't miss with musicians of this caliber.

CHAPTER NINE

Gigs and More Gigs (Busy Times)

Sometime in 1987 I became a member of The Red Onion Jazz Band and for the time being was playing a Sunday gig at The Binghamton Ferry Restaurant, a ferry boat that is permanently docked on the Hudson River in Edgewater, N.J. I played this gig every Sunday afternoon until they let the band go on October 3, 1999. That was a long gig for us.

Also about 1990 Dan Levinson, a clarinetist who was also playing with The Red Onion Jazz Band, was playing the gig at The Cajun Restaurant in New York City. He decided to go to Paris for a year so they made me a permanent member of the band which meant working the New York gig every Saturday. By the way, as of this writing we are still at the Cajun on Saturday nights.

I like working in this band as we use simple charts for structure and there is still room for solos. While the New Orleans revival was going on in Europe it was also going on here in the States. Drummer Bob Thompson formed The Red Onion Jazz Band in 1952. Through the years many well-known players have worked in this band and moved on.

Since I have been playing with this band, which is now a total of 16 years, I and trombonist Dick Dreiwitz have remained permanent members. Larry Weiss on cornet was replaced by Simon Wettenhall. Bob Greene on piano was replaced by Hank Ross. Jack Harkavy on tuba was replaced by Bob Sacchi. Finally, the banjo chair has had the most changes. I have seen Jack Linden, Cynthia Sayer, Richie Lieberson, Alan Cary and, presently, John Gill, a wonderful player who worked with Turk Murphy.

The Red Onion Jazz Band had recorded quite a bit before I joined them. We played a concert at the Watchung Arts Center in April of 1995 and we were recorded. We came out with a CD from that recording. It is called, "Sweet and Hot." It has 15 tunes on it. The personnel on the CD is Larry Weiss, cornet; myself on clarinet and alto sax; Dick Dreiwitz, trombone; Cynthia Sayer, banjo; Hank Ross, piano; Bob Sacchi, tuba and bass sax; and Bob Thompson, drums and Leader.

One Saturday night on April 1, 1992 I arrived at The Cajun to play and discovered I forgot my clarinet at home. I mistakenly took a similar case that had reeds and accessories, and such. I panicked and called local clarinet players and found no one home to get a clarinet to borrow. Dick Miller, who was playing piano that night, had an idea and he called his son who had an alto sax put away in his closet that he didn't play anymore. He brought it in and I put it together and I played it the rest of the night. No one seemed to notice and it actually sounded good. I liked playing it so much that I wound up buying it and have played it ever since.

I don't remember the exact moment I met Cynthia Sayer but I know she was pretty to look at and played the banjo. I must say she was a darn good banjo player and a leader in her own right. I think I met her in the late '80s and called me for a couple of jobs. I started to play with her a lot during 1990 and 1991.

Cynthia got this steady gig every Thursday night at The Fortune Garden Pavilion on 3rd Avenue in New York City. It was a wonderful gig while it lasted which was over a year. I played clarinet and Greg Cohen was on bass and, of course, Cynthia on banjo and vocals. She was a good leader and picked good tunes. We played downstairs and were kind of a warm-up and for the big acts that took place upstairs later on.

During our intermission we would go upstairs and watch the different acts. I got to hear Freddy Cole's Trio, Howard Alden and Ken Peplowski, Dave McKenna, Joanne Brackeen, and others. Sometimes, some of the musicians came down to listen to us during their breaks.

Also, about the same time, she got us this gig at The Honeysuckle, a nice restaurant on Columbus Avenue. We played there on Sunday afternoons. I also remember this Russian clarinetist, Leb Lebedev, who Cynthia invited to sit in with us. He turned out to be a good player and we became good friends and we would sub for each other when one of us got a better gig. What I liked about him (like me) he never held back. He always played with energy and excitement.

It was December 13, 1990 when Cynthia called me to do a jingle in New York at a studio with a 7-piece jazz band for a doctor who owned a bunch of medical offices called Laser Medical Associates. I didn't know what the commercial would be about and didn't really care. In the band she got Peter Ecklund on cornet, Joe Licari on clarinet, Tom Artin on trombone, Arnie Kinsella on drums, Greg Cohen on bass and Cynthia on banjo and Leader. The special guest was trumpeter Byron Stripling who sounded like Louis Armstrong on vocals.

The song we played on the jingle was, "Up The Lazy River." The product was a Hemorrhoid Commercial. Cynthia wrote the commercial and the words that Byron was to talk over our playing. They advertised this number to call 1-800-MD Tusch. They were rectal surgery specialists.

For the last 8 bars of the tune Byron says (in a Louis Armstrong voice), "Get rid of those Hemorrhoid Blues. Call now 'cause you ain't got nothing to lose—except some pain and discomfort—and man, who needs that. Oh, yeah."

I never did another jingle after that. Nothing can beat that one.

In the early 1990s I got to work with so many different bands besides The Red Onions and The Speakeasy Jazz Babies. The Stan Rubin Tigertown Five, at that time, had Randy Reinhart leading the band. He called me for a few gigs and one of them was to do the Pee Wee Stomp.

Randy is always a pleasure to play with and for this event he put together a nice band. Randy, of course, on cornet and myself on clarinet. Tom Artin on trombone and Charlie Harmon, a wonderful sax player. I never worked with him before but his playing reminded me of Eddie Miller. In the rhythm section were Jimmy Andrews on piano and Fred Stoll on drums.

We also did some Cajun gigs on Friday nights in New York City. I also got to work with Bob Greene's World of Jelly Roll Morton. What Bob does is put together a program of Jelly Roll Morton tunes and the band plays things like, "Sweet Substitute," "Kansas City Stomp," and "Big Lip Blues"—all Morton compositions. Bob then tours the States with the band and puts on a show about Ferdinand Jelly Roll Morton.

Mr. Greene, who plays piano in the Morton tradition, has devoted his whole life to bringing the music of Jelly Roll to the awareness of the public. We did a gig at The Harvard Club and in this particular band were Simon Wettenhall on cornet, myself on reeds, Dick Dreiwitz on trombone, Fred Stoll on drums, David Ostwald on tuba, Howard Alden on banjo, singer Ronnie Washam on vocals and Bob Greene, piano and Leader.

There was a club in Westchester that had our kind of music called De Femio's that started a jazz policy. It was a very nice Italian restaurant located on Tuckahoe Road in Yonkers. Al De Femio was a jazz drummer so he would get to play with whomever the artists were that he hired. I believe he had jazz there about 3 days a week. The groups were mostly Quartets, nothing bigger, as the jazz room wasn't that big.

Al promoted good jazz and brought in good jazz artists. Ed Polcer got a few dates there and asked me to play clarinet. Ed used Bobby Pratt on piano. Bobby also played trombone at Jimmy Ryan's with Roy Eldridge on trumpet and Al on drums making it a Quartet. On rare occasions they might have a bass player and would use Bucky Calabrese, a real good player.

Another working band at that time was called, The Lost River Hellcats which had a gig at Jack O'Connor's on Route 22 in Bridgewater, N.J. They played one Friday a month. Jack Harkavy played tuba and was also the Leader. He used John Bucher on cornet and Mike Christianson on trombone. He sometimes used Russ Whitman on clarinet but I believe I did most of the gigs with the band.

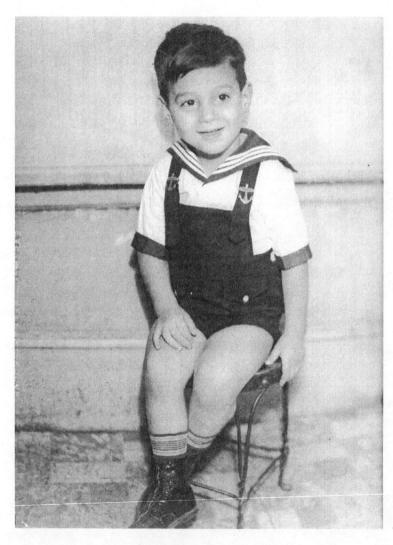

Author—1938

Left to right—Mom and my younger sister. Marie and then
Pop in front of the Sacred Heart Church

1950—Back row: L-R—Nick Fazzolari,
John Mongeluzzo, George Haines

Front row: L-R—Joe Licari—Rocco Fazzolari—
Dom Ippolito

The South Jersey Saints, my first jazz band

Joe Licari, 1957 at Fort Dix, NJ. During basic training.

1959—Shortly after my army discharge

1960—Valerie and I on our wedding day at St. Peters
Church in Haverstraw, N.Y.

Dec. 26, 1966—The King, St. Stompers Performing on NBC Television's Today Show. Hugh Downs and Barbara Walters co—hosted the show. Left to right: Ginny Avery—piano (not shown), Fred Schombert (tenor sax), Joe Licari (clar), George Bailey (tromb), Ed Stanton (trumpet), Kim Blanchard (drums), Al·Wishart (bass).

1971 Ferry boat ride on the Hudson. L—R Barbara Dreiwitz, Dick Roberts, Myself, Herb Randall (back center) Charlie Nuccio.

Myself and Cliff Leeman at "Kilgallens" in Valley Cottage,
NY. 1973.

One of my paintings called "Joe's Jazz Band" 1969.

1973—Legendary trombonist Big Chief Russell Moore and myself at a gig.

1978—The speakeasy Jazz babies at Red Blazer too in New York City

L—R—Front Row Dick Dreiwitz, Myself, Barbara Dreiwitz, John Bucher / L—R—Back row Dick Miller, Richie Barron, Mike Peters, and Betty Comora

The Potomac River Jazz Club Proudly Presents

the

Gully Low Jazz Band

Joe Licari — clarinet	Randy Reinhart — cornet
Dave Ostwald — tuba, leader	Joel Helleny — trombone
Fred Stoll — drums	"Deacon Jim" Lawyer — banjo

The Gully Low Jazz Band was known until recently as the Blazer Bobcats, after the New York jazz club, Red Blazer Too, at which they got their start and still perform regularly. Their musical inspiration leans heavily on Bix's Wolverines and Louis's Hot Five and Hot Seven. In fact, it was Armstrong's seldom-heard tune, "Gully Low Blues," that provided the new name for the band.

POTOMAC ROOM	SATURDAY, JANUARY 10
MARRIOTT TWIN BRIDGES HOTEL	9 PM - 1 AM
SO. END OF 14TH STREET BRIDGE	NO RESERVATIONS
ARLINGTON, VIRGINIA	

ADMISSION: PRJC MEMBERS: $6
NON-MEMBERS: $8

For more information on this and other area jazz activities, Call
532-TRAD

1980 Photo This newley formed band went on the road to
do a few concerts

1985—Photo of my family at our home in Valley Cottage, NY.

1985—Photo of Chuck Slate's Trio from L—R—Chuck Slate, Myself, Hank Ross

1986 Photo L—R—Myself, Bernie Privin, Bob Litwac Back Center

1986—Myself and great trumpeter Doc Cheatham at Jack
O'Conors on drums is Ernie Hackett not shown is Warren
Vache, bass, and Don Coats, Piano

1997—Jim Lowe and friends Back row Jim Lowe, Michael Feinstein (a guest) Bruce McNichols and Dick Voigt—Front row—Barbara Dreiwitz, myself, and Herb Gardner

1998—Palazzo's Restaurant myself and Larry Weiss

The Mississippi Rag ™

September 2000

THE VOICE OF
TRADITIONAL JAZZ AND RAGTIME

**$2.50 U.S.
$3.50 CAN.**

Sacramento Jubilee
Keeps It Fresh

Breaking Records

Flipping Over Phillips

JOE LICARI
An Impressive Body of Work
From an "Invisible" Clarinetist

Photo: Andrew Waterston

The Mississippi Rag is a prestigious journal and jazz voice, and was a honor for me to make there front cover. Many thanks to writer Joe Klee and Leslie Johnson, the editor.

March 2000 At the Algonquin in NYC. Featuring Julie
Wilson, Smith Street Society Jazz Band L—R myself, Herb
Gardner, Julie Wilson, Barbara Dreiwitz, Bruce McNicholas.

2002 Big Apple Jazz Band at Cajun Restaurant in NYC.
L—R. Front row—Tom Artin, John Bucher, myself, Back
Row—Kevin Dorn, Dick Waldburger, Marty Grosz, Dick
Voigt.

2003 The Red Onion Jazz Band at the Watchung Art Center. Front Row—L—R—Myself, Bob Sacchi Back Row—L—R—Simon Wettenhall, Bob Thompson, Dick Dreiwitz, John Gill, Hank Ross.

On piano he had Steve Knight who also played other instruments, including trombone and tuba. Marty Sobel was on banjo and Co-leader. The vocalist was Carol Leigh, a wonderful singer, whom I had worked with before. This was a nice band that should have worked more but as is usually the case there are more bands out there than there is work.

The Ridgewood Library in New Jersey had a jazz spectacular that was held annually and we played for its 17th Annual Concert. Besides the Hellcats, we had to play opposite Ed Polcer's Dixieland All-Stars. He had a great band that day, too. I had worked before with everybody in Polcer's band except for the clarinetist Ken Peplowkski, whom I had met before, and drummer Tom Melito.

After the concert was over Ed Polcer announced that both bands were coming out on stage for a Jam Session. The combined bands played, "That's A-Plenty" for the finale. Also in Polcer's band that day was Vince Giordano, Tom Artin, John Halsey and I played clarinet. Ken Peplowski was gracious enough to switch to tenor sax for the last tune. I was happy about that as Ken's clarinet playing is intimidating to me as he is so good that he is rated as one of the top clarinetists today.

I remember doing this gig with Polcer but I think the leader that day was Phil Sasson, a trombone player, and also Brian Nalepka on string bass. During one of his bass solos, with Brian playing enthusiastically with a huge booming sound, I looked over to Polcer and said, "Sounds like, "Big Noise From Nalepka." We all laughed about it afterwards, except Brian.

I told that story to a few musicians and they told me to send it to Bill Crow for his column, The Crow's Nest, which Bill does for Local 802. I called him up, he liked it, and it was put in his column.

On Sundays when I would go play on the ferry boat with the Red Onion Band I would pass this club called, Struggles, which was in Edgewater, New Jersey not far from where I played. I heard they had a lot of good jazz being played there on weekends. It had different kinds of jazz and sometimes it was traditional. Mickey Gravine, who was a trombone player, ran the music but I believe his sister owned the place. He was a good player but I think he was more big band oriented than a dixieland kind of player. If you didn't know where this place was you would never find it. There was no sign outside advertising the place and it was on the second story of an apartment house.

It wasn't a very big place and he advertised by a word of mouth sort of thing. The room was long with the stage at one end and the bar at the other end with a few tables in between. Polcer called me to play the weekend there with him that Friday and Saturday and he put together a great band. Besides Ed and myself and Mickey Gravine, he brought in John Bunch on piano and Frank Tate on bass plus a new kid on drums named Joe Ascione. This kid could really play well and today he is in great demand at all the big festivals. This was some band Polcer put together and it was a weekend I won't soon forget.

We got the sad news of my Mom's passing on August 16, 1992. My mother lived to the ripe age of 92 years young. She lived in Florida for the last 25 years very near to where my sister Jeanne lived who had moved to Florida seeking the warmer climate for one of her children who had severe sinus problems at the time.

Mom never re-married when Pop died and lived on her own very independently as she never wanted to be a burden on anyone. Jeanne always looked in on her every day and took her food shopping or for doctor's visits when needed. Mom was in pretty good shape for her years and occasionally needed a little help here and there.

An unfortunate thing happened to Mom one day as she sat in the back of the car being taken somewhere when another car slammed them from behind. The impact caused Mom to break several bones, both of her wrists, her nose and several vertebrae in the chest. She was in the hospital for months trying to heal and was in much pain. At that age you don't heal well and eventually she lost the will to live.

Who knows, she may have lived to see 100 years if not for the accident. My sister Jeanne and her family had a one day viewing and the next day the body was sent to Vineland, N.J. so she could be buried next to my father.

Lev Lebedev, the Russian clarinetist, was going back to Russia. I had met Lev a couple of years before when I was playing with Cynthia Sayer's band. Lev sat in and we liked each other's playing right away. He was always my first call sub after that. He played a lot like me and I liked that.

By now, Lev was the clarinetist with the Washboard Kings at the Cajun on Tuesday nights. He was having a problem with Immigration for overstaying his visa. They tried to get him to stay as Stan King, the Leader of the band, would vouch for him and guarantee he had a job. Lev decided to go back to Russia and did very well there as jazz is received much better throughout Europe than here.

Stan King threw a big going away party for Lev at The Cajun Restaurant in NYC. Most of the local jazz players that worked with Lev came out to wish him well and to jam with him. Just to name a few who came: Peter Ecklund, Lee Lorenz, Simon Wettenhall, Ed Polcer, Jon Erik Kelso, Frank Driggs, Joe Licari, Joe Muranyi, Dick Dreiwitz, Paul Bacon, Bob Greene, Dick Voigt, John Halsey, Eddy Davis, Alan Cary, Barbara Dreiwitz, Brian Nalepka, Bob Thompson and Giampaolo Biagi.

A wonderful time was had by all—Farewell to Lev.

I must say that next to Bob Wilber, Kenny Davern is another hero of mine who I got to know through the years. I don't know if its true but someone told me once that Kenny said that I was the best clarinetist of all the part-timers playing around the NYC area. If Kenny did indeed say that to someone, that's fine, as I respect his playing very much. The only thing I take exception with is I never regarded myself as full time or part-time, but a jazz clarinet player who tried very hard to make a difference by being out there as much as I could playing this music we love.

I figured out that I probably played more gigs a month than so-called "full time" musician s. I envied those who went away to do all the special parties and festivals and made a name for themselves. Somebody had to stay behind and do the dirty work so I tried to establish myself in the Tri-State area playing with as many jazz bands as I could.

Kenny is the only clarinet player who has ever called me to sub for him. This says two things to me: That I must be a good player and, I pose no threat to him but got the job done. I like the latter best. I must clarify that when I say no one called me to sub for them, I mean clarinetists of Kenny's caliber, which is the highest. Kenny called me again to fill in for him like he had done once before for the Cornerstone gig. This time he gave me a couple of great paying gigs that he couldn't do as he was going away and recommended me again to Tony De Nicola, the wonderful drummer who worked with the Harry James Orchestra.

Tony had this big benefit for St., Jude's Children's Research Hospital which took place at a hotel in New Brunswick, New Jersey. Marlo Thomas, Danny Thomas's daughter, was there to represent her dad who had recently passed. There were other celebrities and musical acts.

We played in the hallway entrance for a set and later inside in the ballroom. Tony always puts together a good band so I got to work with the likes of Jon Erik Kelso, Joel Helleny, John Bunch, Murray Wall and, of course, Tony.

Except for me, all these guys are big names in Jazz.

I'm just recalling a Kenny Davern story and remember playing at Michael's Pub subbing for Woody Allen. In the audience were Kenny Davern and Dick Wellstood who came in for a few drinks. After the set Kenny invited us over for a drink and was surprised to see me instead of Woody. He gave me a big kiss on the cheek and said I sounded great. I think he was sincere—or was that the drink talking?

One time I called Kenny and asked if he had any plastic clarinets as I was looking for something to play outdoors and I know Kenny has played plastic clarinets before. He had this one clarinet called, "The Graduate," which I never heard of, and he said he would send it for me to try. This clarinet was in very good shape and played and had the feel of a better clarinet like my Selmer. I had a new Bundy that someone gave me but it never felt comfortable to play as my fingers always felt too big to finger on it. Anyway, Kenny's clarinet worked out quite well for me and

I mainly now have it set up ready to play for practicing purposes in my bedroom.

Arthur's Tavern, on Grove Street in New York's Greenwich Village, is a wonderful place to go to hear Dixieland Jazz. On Monday nights you can hear, The Grove Street Stompers led by Bill Dunham on piano. He wins the award for having the longest running gig in New York City—over 30 years.

A long time friend and cornetist, Lee Lorenz, is the Leader of The Creole Cooking Jazz Band that plays there every Sunday night. He can boast being there over 20 years. Lee plays hot cornet and doesn't hold back. Ernie Lumer is the clarinetist with this band and for the last few years, up to date, I sub for him the last Sunday of the month only. I always wanted to ask Ernie why he always takes off at the end of the month but figured it's none of my business and I don't want to lose the gig. I also get to play with my good friend, Dick Dreiwitz, who is on trombone, Skip Muller on bass, Steve Elmer on piano and Ed Bonoff on drums.

This one reply I got from Bob Wilber was to thank me for sending him some pieces of rubber which you cut to size and stick to the back of the mouthpiece. I had a lot of this rubber as I've used it for years. I think it gives you better control and your teeth don't cut into the mouthpiece scarring it. Also, it opens up the throat giving you a better sound.

I discovered that Bob used the rubber backing when I first took lessons from him. I thought I was the only one doing this. He only uses it on his saxophones now.

He mentioned that he was doing a CD for Arbors Records with four tenor saxes which was a Salute to Coleman Hawkins. Besides Bob, were Harry Allen, Anti Sarpilla and Tommy Whittle. He also enclosed a copy of his book, "Music Was Not Enough," which I believe you could only get in England. It's a great autobiography and I have read it a few times as I always find I missed something the read before. I recommend it to all the clarinet players out there. I learned a lot about Wilber that I never knew.

In the book he sent me he had a nice inscription which reads: "To my friend, Joe—a fine student who has come a long way. I only teach the best! Keep it up." Bob Wilber.

A couple of months later I got another letter from Wilber and he mentioned his Salute to Hawkins went well and that they all got different sounds on their tenors which makes it interesting. He mentioned his next project for Arbors with the rhythm section of Ralph Sutton and Bucky Pizzarelli, Bob Haggart and Butch Miles. Bob was going to concentrate on the straight soprano on this one as well as his Buescher altos, which are a little earlier than mine but the same model.

I must have sent him a tape to listen to but can't remember what it was and he wrote, "I listened to your tape this AM. Your clarinet sounds wonderful, a bit like early Benny with touches of Pee-Wee." Then, he got serious with me and we became teacher and student again as he continues to write, "I think all of us involved in playing traditional jazz must strive to create some new sounds, within the idiom, otherwise our efforts invariably suffer when compared with the original recordings. What do you think?"

Something tells me that he started out by giving me a compliment and in the next few lines he took it away!!

Lee Lorenz, cartoonist for The New Yorker, art editor and musician, had this wonderful gig at Columbia University. Lee used me on clarinet and we played for the Fraternity a couple of times a year. This lasted for about four years or so as the head of the music program graduated and we lost the gig. The kids loved us and the dance floor was packed with hundreds of kids and large lines outside waiting to come in. We always had a good band and if Lee couldn't make it we used Jon Eric Kelso, John Bucher or Ed Polcer on cornet. Piano chair was usually Dick Voigt or Keith Ingham. Skip Muller on bass and Ed Bonoff, drums.

The kids seemed to know the music and requested good tunes. I would ask some of the kids how they knew this music and they would always say their parents liked it and they grew up hearing it in the house. Playing for these kids made me think about how it must have been when jazz flourished and kids danced in the aisles at the Paramount Theater listening to the Benny Goodman band. These kids were polite, nicely dressed in suits and the young ladies in pretty dresses and at the end of the gig would come up to us and thank us for coming and tell us how much they enjoyed our music. That was a quality gig that I wish we still had as we could have gotten to a lot of kids to perpetuate our music.

CHAPTER TEN

Free at Last (Time for Growth)

The years from 1996 to the present have been very fulfilling. Not having a day gig anymore, I now have more time to play, do recordings and write some new songs. Dick Voigt, a great piano player who plays in the Gene Schroeder tradition, started his own band and called it, "The Big Apple Jazz Band." We play the Condon-style dixieland which we all love with blends of New Orleans and Chicago styles.

Our first big job was playing at the Helen Hayes Performing Arts Center in Nyack, NY. We did a concert called, 52nd Street Revisited. In the band at that time was Ed Polcer, Tom Artin, myself on reeds, Skip Muller, Giampaolo Biagi and great vocalist Stella Marrs. The Edward Hopper House promotes, "Jazz In The Garden" and we did a concert for them. This time the band changed slightly with Warren Vaché on cornet and Dick Waldburger on bass. And no vocalist on this one.

The following year we went back to perform at the Helen Hayes Theater and this time we did a concert for the Martin Luther King Center, After School Program and Dick produced the whole show. He asked the great reed player, Benny Waters, to join us and the great bass player, Leonard Gaskin, Polcer, myself, Dreiwitz and Biagi completed the band—and what a band it was!

Waters was superb and played like a young man even though at this time he was over 90 years of age and blind. Most of these concerts we did were recorded so Voigt took the featured highlights from these live performances and produced a CD. He chose not to use any with Waters on it and I think he should have. Benny Waters passed away a few months later.

Dick Voigt and I recently did a duo at the Rockland Conservatory of Music. Our theme that day was a 5-City Musical Tour. We did 5 tunes with a different city in the title. We went over very well. We were the jazz segment, as well as classical music, that was performed that day.

Dick got us a steady Sunday gig at the Cajun Restaurant and the band did real good the first few weeks. We lasted for five months and they let us go as there was not enough business to support a 7-piece band. We had a great band but people just don't come out Sunday nights probably because they work the next day. John Bucher was on cornet, myself on reeds, Tom Artin on trombone, Marty Grosz on guitar, Dick Waldburger on bass and young Kevin Dorn on drums. Kevin was all of 21 years of age and is going to be a great drummer some day. Dick was using Kevin quite a bit there for a while and got a call to join Jim Cullum's band in San Antonio, Texas. Kevin is young and this was a good break for him. The band plays full time and is a well established jazz band. They do a radio show, do concerts and play every night at The Landing.

Which reminds me that Jim Cullum asked me about 3 years ago if I was interested in joining his band as Evan Christopher was leaving. I was flattered and asked how he got my name. He said Jon Eric Kelso recommended me. I refused as although it's a great band, it's a strict, regimented kind of a band and I need more freedom. Besides, I hate hot weather.

The Big Apple Jazz Band started a new steady gig at O'Connor's Restaurant in Watchung, New Jersey. We had the same personnel except Steve Little was now playing drums. The gig was short lived as not enough people were coming out and the owner was charging $25 a person for a special menu. Not counting drinks, you're looking at serious money. Old people can't afford that kind of money on a fixed income. Anyway, we lasted a whole 6 weeks.

We just played the Pee Wee Stomp for the second time with this band and were well received. Dick belongs to a lot of causes like The Family Shelter, Abused Women, and Halfway House for recovering alcoholics. He is also involved in politics. He has a lot on his plate and does a lot of good for people. When the band works for all these organizations, Dick takes no money for himself but pays us well. He is a good guy and a good friend and a good musician.

Sometime in 1999 I wrote Bob Wilber and asked if he had a curved soprano he wanted to sell as I wanted to start playing it to add to the arsenal, so to speak. Bob said he didn't but recommended me to his friend in California by the name of Hank Thorp who sold reed instruments to the top players only.

I called him and asked him if he had anything I could try. He had 3 horns to send me all in great shape and would send them out to me. He sent a Buescher, and a Pan American and a Conn. I fell in love with the Conn as it had the best tone and felt easy to play. I bought the Conn and I let Wilber know what I got. It winds up that Bob played a Conn curved also except his was a 1922 gold plated and mine is silver plated, around 1925 model.

Hank Thorp also found a similar horn for Paul Chernon, a student Wilber had from France who has a band called, The Tuxedo Big Band. Wilber eventually recorded a nice CD with them doing Fletcher Henderson arrangements that Benny Goodman never recorded. Bob said Anti Sarpilla plays one of his old horns as well as Luca Vellotti who also were his students. Anti from Denmark and Luca from Italy.

I actually met Luca at a Pee Wee Stomp I was playing at and he was in the audience. He introduced himself and we became friends and wrote to each other for awhile. He sent me some music of his and he is a good player. I once suggested to Bob of maybe doing a recording of all his students playing together. He thought it was an interesting idea, but nothing came of it.

In May of 1999 I got a call that my brother Andy had a fatal heart attack at age 72. It was hard to comprehend as no one in our family has a history of coronary problems. Then we find a couple of years later both my older sister and brother had bypasses and are fine now. So, who knows why these things happen. I try to take care of myself and keep the cholesterol down, exercise, and stay away from junk foods. What else can one do?

Larry Weiss, who is a lyrical cornet player in the Hackett tradition, also is a fine piano player. Sometime in early 1998 he was doing a single at Palazzo's Restaurant in Montclair, N.J. and talked the owner into hiring me on clarinet to form a duo. I started there in May of 1998 just about the same time they were running the Montclair Blues and Jazz Festival, which I believe was its 13th that year. What they would do is have a camera man go around the clubs and video the different acts and put it on cable.

The Montclair Times gave us a nice write-up and said, "Weiss and Licari bring a swing sound to the festival that will keep the audience on their toes. Expect to hear Benny Goodman and Teddy Wilson favorites in their repertoire. Joe Licari has also been known to fill in for Woody Allen at Michael's Pub in New York City."

Larry and I have been at Palazzo's since 1998 to present which is going on five years. We are there most Fridays and some Saturdays. We are on our second owner now and get along great with everyone there.

People at the restaurant enjoy our music and are very complimentary. I sold some of my CDs there but they would ask if Larry and I had one together. So we went to a studio and got our friends John Maimone and Bob Speiden to record us. I'm glad we made it and think it's a pretty good recording. We sell them at Palazzo's and when people ask us if we have a CD we smile and point to the CDs on the piano.

Larry and I enjoy playing there very much and we get to play wonderful ballads by wonderful composers like Berlin, Rogers and Hart, Gershwin, Ellington and many others. We also get other work from people who hear us and hire us for their affairs.

In 2002 I wrote two more songs and also did the lyrics. One is called, "I'll Dream of You" which I think is a lovely ballad. Of all my tunes I like this and "Haunting Melody" the best. I also wrote a song called "Julie" which I will explain more about later on.

I always liked getting a letter from Bob Wilber as they were constructive as well as instructive. He once wrote the following, "Thanks for the cassette—had to wait a long time for your soprano but it sounds good, very in tune. My only suggestion would be to try for more intensity. I think Bechet was too intense sometimes, but the soprano should be a powerful and dramatic instrument. Too many players sound like a bad oboe! I get a lot of inspiration from listening to Louis' Hot Five."—

A few months later I received another reply from Bob. "Thanks for the tape. I think you're coming along fine on the soprano and it sounds like you've been listening to Louis, which is great. He is the foundation on which everything was built! I'd like to hear you on ballads and blues with more sustained notes. That's when vibrato becomes so important."

CHAPTER ELEVEN

Radio Days (Stories from the Stars)

He talked about some other things and ended by saying the following, "Keep up the good work, Joe, and remember the three things that count: Sing, Swing, and make a personal statement. Amen."

About 1997 radio station WVNJ, 1160 AM in Teaneck, New Jersey inaugurated the Jim Lowe and Friends Show. Former WNEW disk jockey Jim Lowe, who had a hit record with, "The Green Door" way back in 1956, picked Bruce McNichols leader of The Smith Street Society Jazz Band to head the house band on the show. I must say that prior to working with Jim Lowe we worked with Ted Brown doing radio remotes from different places until he became ill and went to a nursing home to recuperate.

Ted Brown also was a disk jockey on the old WNEW radio station. Ted Brown never returned so Jim Lowe continued doing the show. Bruce McNichols picked the following to be in the house band: trombonist Herb Gardner, tubaist Barbara Dreiwitz, pianist Dick Voigt, and myself on clarinet and saxophones. We did a live show on WVNJ every Sunday morning with the most unbelievable guests one can imagine. I looked forward to every show. Every show was recorded and I have all the shows on tape and now CD's. I have many photos that were taken with the guests.

The first few shows we did we had Margaret Whiting, Julius La Rosa, Jerry Vale, Barbara Cook, and Maureen McGovern. Each guest got about 30 minutes and they would be interviewed and they would sing either with the house band or they brought their own accompaniment, which was mostly the case. Some of the jazz musicians who were on as guests were Les Paul, Red Richards, Dick Hyman, Bucky Pizzarelli, Howard Alden, Ken Peplowski and Sam Butera.

We also booked a lot of cabaret stars like K. T. Sullivan, Jeff Harner, Eric Comstock, Daryl Sherman, and Julie Wilson. After a year or so the station changed to a more contemporary format. Jim Lowe and his program director Bill Gaghan quit over this decision and are now part of a syndicated series which tapes live at the Museum of Television and Radio at 25 West 52nd Street in New York City. Tapings generally happen on the second Wednesday of each month beginning at 11:00 AM and ending at 3:00 PM. Live audiences are invited and encouraged.

One of my favorite guests has been Tony Martin. He was on our show January 31, 1998 and he was a great guest with lots of stories. He was born Alvin Morris in San Francisco. He claims he and Humphrey Bogart were born on Christmas Day. After graduating from St. Mary's College he had thought about going to law school but decided to become a professional musician. He played clarinet and saxophone.

He joined the Tom Gerun Orchestra and in the same band was Woody Herman. Tony eventually became Woody's best man. Someone asked Tony, "How did you become a singer?"

He replied, "Someone heard me play the saxophone, so I became a singer."

Tony Martin said one day with the band he sang, Poor Butterfly and someone heard him and before he knew it he was in Hollywood working in a musical with the likes of Fred Astaire and Ginger Rogers. He called his mother to give her the good news and she replied, "Tony, you've been drinking again?"

He told this story about singer Ginny Simms. Tom Gerun's orchestra needed a singer and heard about Ms. Simms singing in Fresno. He sent Tony Martin and Woody Herman to hear her and if she was good to hire her. They went down and were racing through town and were stopped by a policeman.

They said, "What did I do officer?"

The policeman said, "You were doing 48 miles an hour."

Tony said, "This car can't do 48 miles an hour."

He proceeded to explain that he was here to audition some girl called Virginia Simms.

The cop said,"follow me. She's my daughter."

How's that for coincidence?

Another great guest was Steve Allen who was on the show on February 21, 1998. Steve was plugging his new book, "Die Laughing," a murder mystery. He also had a video out called, "Steve Allen's 75th Birthday Celebration" showing a hilarious musical trip through a half century career with a lot of guests. Steve was asked to play the piano and chose one of his compositions called, "I Remember Spring in Maine." He mentioned while playing the song that, singer and lyric writer, Carol Leigh heard it and called him up. She told Steve how much she loved the song and would like to do the lyrics for it—which she did.

Steve talked about, "The Benny Goodman Story" and about Benny Goodman himself. Steve and Jim Lowe were trading Benny stories and once Jim Lowe interviewed Benny and asked about, "The Ray."

Benny said, "That really is sometimes a compliment. I'm standing there in awe"!! (Yeah, hoping that they hit a clinker.)

Benny was known to have a bad memory so one time he called up musicologist George Simon and Benny says, "George, it's embarrassing but I can never remember your wife's name."

So George said, "Her name is Blanche."

Benny said, "OK, thanks Bob."

Benny once introduced a white piano player as Teddy Wilson because he couldn't think of his name.

Steve Allen invited Benny on his television show to promote the movie. Benny was to come out, talk about the picture, then they would play a little something on the clarinet.

When it was over, Steve said, "That was great, Benny."

Benny couldn't think of Steve's name and said, "Awe, thanks, Pops."

He also mentioned how great it was to hang out with Teddy Wilson, Gene Krupa and Lionel Hampton while making the picture. Clarinetist Sol Yaged became Steve Allen's coach. He taught Steve how to hold the clarinet, take it apart and put it together again.

Steve said one time when doing a show on WNEW-AM a caller asked him if he had any children. Steve said, "Well, yes, Jane and I have two beautiful children and one ugly one." Steve Allen was having such a good time on the Jim Lowe show that he hung around.

Also a guest that day was The Red Onion Jazz Band. We got Steve to sit in with the band which was great. After the show was over Steve was gracious enough to take a picture with me holding my clarinet.

The great pianist George Shearing was our radio guest on February 28, 1998. He is a funny guy with puns and lots of stories. He mentioned how he spends six months out of the year in England and lives in the middle of the country with lots of cows surrounding his house.

One morning he went outside and said to the cows, "You sure are making a racket out here today. What do you think of Duke Ellington? Do you know the old, "Moo Indigo?"

Jim Lowe said to George he remembers meeting him in Chicago when playing the Chicago Theater. George replies, "I believe Patti Page was also on the show singing those wonderful songs, "Tennessee Waltz" and "How Much Is That Guide Dog In The Window?"

Mr. Shearing happened to be in town to do a concert at the 92nd Street Y with Dick Hyman. He said that he thought Dick, with maybe the possible exception of Hank Jones, did a wonderful impression of Art Tatum. He told him he should do an album and call it, "Hyman on a Tatum Pole."

Early in George Shearing's career, he worked in the bands of Jack Hylton and Bert Ambrose, both English bands. He started playing accordion in an all-blind band and all the parts were in Braille. Their theme song was, "I'll See You In My Dreams" and they played Jimmy Lunceford arrangements.

He told Mr. Lowe, "A true gentleman is a man who knows how to play the accordion, and doesn't."

George continued with, "I knew a man who was so in love with his accordion. He was devastated one night to find out that he had left his accordion in the car unlocked. He couldn't wait for the evening to be over so he could get back to his car to see if the accordion was still there. To his great relief, the accordion was still there; plus, two other accordions and three banjos."

George Shearing is a giant on piano and a wonderful human being.

Singer Jerry Vale was on the Jim Lowe Show on May 10, 1997. Jim Lowe reminded Jerry where they first met. It had been in Cleveland in 1956.

"I remember I had a hit with, "The Green Door," and you had a big hit at that time. We were waiting to see Bill Randall, and waiting ahead of us were Nat Cole and Patti Page."

The story goes that Patti Page was working somewhere for an older crowd. She began working the room and as she passed the table of this older gentleman, he tried to pass her a $10 bill and she said, "Don't do that anymore."

He talked of Frank Sinatra and Mel Tormé. That they were very sick and he visited both of them. He thought Frank seemed to be getting better at the time as he started picking on everybody—which is a good sign. As for Mel, he had a stroke and was just holding his own and we are all praying for him.

Jerry talked a lot about Tony Bennett, and that he was responsible for opening doors for himself and singers like Jack Jones and Steve Lawrence, due to Tony's association with K. D. Lang. He said Tony is a beautiful guy and totally dedicated to his craft, and is the nicest human being you'll ever meet in your life.

As the conversation continued they talked of birthdays. Jim Lowe had mentioned that he and Bob Barker were born on the same day and each year on that day they would call each other.

Jerry Vale interrupted by saying, "It's funny but Steve Lawrence and myself were born on July 8th and no matter where we are in the world, we call each other. We have been doing this for 30 years."

He talked about how fortunate he was to be in the music business.

"I like to sing. I never studied voice or took lessons. I can read music a little bit but I'm not schooled in music. I'm blessed with a good ear. I learn songs very fast and have recorded with the best musicians in the world. I'm blessed and thank God every day of my life."

At one time, Jerry Vale used to live in Englewood, N.J. and then he moved to Tenafly. N.J.

"I got this gig working for the Howard Hughes organization in Las Vegas doing 22 weeks a year. I moved my young family to Vegas for about 10 years. Then Hughes died and that was the end of the gig. I moved to Beverly Hills, CA.

I have wonderful friends here, people like Hugh Heffner. I go to his mansion a couple of times a week and we watch movies. The days of Bunny's and girls walking around with skimpy clothes— that's over,

Jimmy Roselli has been a guest before and is a man who speaks his mind. The last time he was on was September 15, 2001.

Jim Lowe says, "You look good, Jimmy."

In which Mr. Roselli replies, "I feel good, Jim, considering I've had four by-passes, a pacemaker and am living on pills."

Jimmy Roselli grew up in Hoboken, New Jersey and to this day has a house overlooking Hoboken, where he spends most of his time.

He was asked about Frank Sinatra and had a lot to say about him.

"As you know, Frank was also from Hoboken and I would see him from time to time as we lived a few houses from each other. Once he invited me to his house as he heard I had this great range in my singing. He had this piano in the house and I thought he was going to play it but all he did was play a single note scale so he could hear my range, and that was it."

"To be honest, Frank and I never got along. He was a great talent but very insecure. One day he has his arm around you and the next day he wants to kill you. He was like a Jeckel and Hyde."

One time Jimmy asked Gordon Jenkins, "How do you put up with this guy, Sinatra?"

Gordon replied, "I stay away from him."

Jimmy Roselli likes to make money, he says, but sometimes it's hard to convince the people who want to hire you. One time someone wanted him to play this small theater and asked Mr. Roselli. When told the theater only had 300 seats Mr. Roselli said, "Then, you can't afford me."

I would tell them, "You want a Rolls Royce and want to pay with a Ford pocketbook."

Jimmy has a wonderful book out called, "Making the Wise Guys Weep—The Jimmy Roselli Story," by David Evanier. Also, there is a movie being made of his life, so watch for it.

The Smith Street Society Jazz Band of the Jim Lowe Radio Show sometimes backed up stars of Broadway and Cabaret who showed up for guest appearances. Julie Wilson, the Queen of all the cabaret stars, liked the way the band played behind her and conceived of an idea to create a show called, "Julie Wilson in Dixieland."

Her accompanist, Mark Hummel on piano, was to do all the arrangements. We had a few rehearsals at Barbara Dreiwitz's house and Julie's manager, Ron Cohn, booked us into the Oak Room of The Algonquin on 44th Street for five weeks. We went in February 2nd to March 4th, 2000 and did 16 wonderful shows with Julie. They loved Julie, backed by a Dixieland band, and we went over big with full houses most of the time.

We were a hit and Rex Reed for the New York Observer did a big article on Julie Wilson and the band. He titled it, Mardi Gras in Manhattan. The whole article was much too long but I will give some of the highlights:

"The svelte, sobbing sophistication of Julie Wilson and the free-form-down-calico noodling of Dixieland, do not automatically seem to be a dream match, but her new cabaret act at the Algonquin, a festive free-for-all called, Julie Wilson in Dixieland, euphoria reigns triumphant."

"Not since the days of Eddie Condon's Dixieland Jazz emporium have the Saint's come marching in with such a blast. She shimmies, she shakes, she melts you like bayou honeysuckle."

From, "Darktown Strutters Ball" to "Won't You Come Home Bill Bailey," Julie Wilson investigates every nuance of the Dixieland style, captivating her audience and proving, once again, why her musical prowess is like a master class for performers and audiences alike."

CHAPTER TWELVE

Julie Wilson (Queen of Cabaret)

We recorded the show for a CD the last night at the Algonquin and we were paid as sidemen. It was to come out in a few months. Then we were told, because of internal problems with the record company and other things, it would not be released. Too bad, and maybe someone will come along and produce it one day.

Our association did not end here by any means and we wound up doing a whole series of things in the next year or two, thanks to the wonderful reviews, like one written in The New York Times by Stephen Holden:

"Accompanied by the Smith Street Society Jazz Band, a Dixieland quartet (banjo, tuba, trombone and clarinet), augmented by her Musical Director Mark Hummel on piano, Ms. Wilson wittily takes on the role of New Orleans-style Red-Hot Mama twirling her different colored boas. From the opening number, in which the band parades into the Oak Room of the Algonquin Hotel, maintains a festive party atmosphere.

Then, in October of the same year, we were booked at the Pace Theater Downtown, for a concert called, Jack Kleinsinger presents, "Highlights In Jazz" with Julie Wilson and the Smith Street Society Jazz Band. That's a nice theater and I believe I only played there once before a few years ago. That night we played opposite the Freddy Cole Quartet. Freddy and I had met before when I was playing at The Fortune Garden with banjoist Cynthia Sayer. Freddy Cole is a fine singer and piano player.

Then, later on that month we did the 11th Annual New York Cabaret Convention at Town Hall on West 43rd Street. We had a couple of rehearsals before hand as Julie Wilson insisted on that, even though we did it many times before. You get to improve it more each time.

Every major Cabaret star was there that night, such as Christine Andreas, Andrea Marcovici, Wesla Whitfield, K.T. Sullivan, and special guest star that night was the still lovely Celeste Holm. She was wonderful in the movie High Society co-starring with Bing, Frank and Grace Kelly.

I didn't work for Julie Wilson again till about 6 months later. How that all came about was Barbara Dreiwitz had mentioned to me she was going to San Francisco with Julie to do the same show over there. Except for Barbara, the other musicians would get hired over there, as to save all those plane fares, by not taking the Smith Street Society Jazz Band to do it.

I asked Barbara if she can mention me for the clarinet chair as I would love to work with Julie again and besides I knew the arrangements by heart. I then got a call from Julie's Manager, Ron Cohn, who told me Julie and Mark Hummel on piano and Musical Director, would love me to work with them. We talked about the accommodations, plane fare, salary, etc. I agreed to go and was excited as I never went to San Francisco before. When the time came we all met at the airport and flew on Continental on June 14, 2001.

When we arrived we were taken by limousine to the York Hotel on Sutter Street and all our engagements were to be held in the same hotel in the Plush Room which was on the first floor in the back of the hotel. The hotel was beautiful and the accommodations were first class. We had two rehearsals and the engagement officially started on June 19 through July 1, and fly back on the 2nd.

I must say I fell in love with San Francisco. We had plenty of time off for sight seeing and found great food in Chinatown. We walked everywhere and by the time I left I was in good shape from all the hills. Also, the weather is just perfect there. The gig was great and working with Julie is always fun. She treated Barbara Dreiwitz and I like family.

On our days off we would sometimes get together and Julie

would take us all out for dinner and she would pick up the tab. She was that way in other situations, also. She is a very generous lady. We played for full houses most of the time and the show, "Julie Wilson in Dixieland" got good reviews. Some of the headlines of the articles read, "Lusty Ladies Fill Wilson's Musical World," "Have Boa, Will Travel," Wilson "Dixie-Style Cabaret."

The musicians backing up Julie were the superb pianist Mark Hummel who wrote the arrangements, and his New Orleans-style band featuring Marty Wahner on trombone and myself on clarinet, Barbara Dreiwitz on tuba and an old friend John Gill on banjo, whom we recommended.

The gig finally ended and we flew back to New York.

The Hideaway on 37th Street where I had played before with the Tigertown Five was trying to generate new business as it wasn't doing well and got the idea to try cabaret. The room where I had played in jazz bands was now changed to The Hideaway Cabaret & Supper Club. They called the room, "The Julie Wilson Room." If you are going to name a room why not after the very best in cabaret? There was a lot of promotion, etc.

They wrote of Miss Wilson, "We feel that since Miss Wilson has given so much support to the cabaret community over the years and helped define the art form with her dazzling performances, this honor is overdue as well deserved."

It opened officially on September 5, 2001 and we were right there with her once again. The Smith Street Society was asked to play and we worked there for four days with Julie to start it off. There were other performers besides Julie, like Lanie Kazan, K.T. Sullivan, and Larry Woodard. The next night there was Dave Frishberg, Barbara Carroll, Margaret Whiting, and each night some one different. As wonderful as all this sounds it never made much of a difference as business was not good, and soon after they closed the place for good.

There's something to be said for, Location, Location, Location. And I'm sure the disaster of the Twin Towers on September 1, 2001 didn't help, either.

We next worked with Julie again at the Algonquin for New

Year's Eve and that was to be the last time we would work together. I liked meeting and playing with Cabaret Artists. I found them interesting and dedicated and no big egos, and very friendly. I found it to be a good learning experience. I would like to work with Julie again someday.

To show my gratitude for my association with Ms. Wilson I wrote a song and lyrics called, "Julie." I sent it to her and have not yet gotten a reply whether she liked it or hated it. WILL KEEP YOU POSTED!

I have Joe H. Klee to thank for caring enough to do an article about me in, The Mississippi Rag. I made the front page with my picture and the caption read, "Joe Licari, An Impressive Body of Work from an Invisible Clarinetist." Mr. Klee wrote a wonderful biography that spread over six pages with a lot of photos. The is a very prestigious magazine that goes all over the world. You will find this article in the September, 2000 issue, for anyone interested.

It took me almost 50 years to get this kind of recognition, and it's nice to see our life's work in print for all to see and be proud of. That's one of the reasons I'm writing this book for other musicians like myself. who have devoted their whole life to playing our wonderful music—and nobody knows them.

My only sin for being invisible is the fact that I never had the opportunity to travel like the well known musicians. Playing mostly in the New York area has been my life, and stood close to home, and yet I was born at the wrong time, I feel I am too young for the old timers I listened to as a kid and I'm too old for the youngsters coming up now. That's the way it is today. The young ones stay together as a clique, working with the same people all the time and people like me get excluded instead of included and I can play as well as most of them. It's true that I do lack reading skills and I would never be able to work in Vince Giordano's band. But would love to if I could.

There are other musicians in New York who should be better known like Bob Kindred, Dan Block, Paul Lindemeyer, who are all excellent reed players; and Hank Ross, Bob Greene on piano; and trombone players like Tom Artin, Herb Gardner, Richard

Dreiwitz; and cornet players John Bucher, Larry Weiss, and Lee Lorenz, just to name a few. And there are many more on other instruments.

There are also old established jazz bands no one writes about like, The Red Onion Jazz Band, The Speakeasy Jazz Babies, The Creole Cooking Jazz Band and The Grove Street Stompers.

All the bands are New York based and have played the Tri-State area for over 40 years. It's interesting how I have stayed so invisible all these years, yet visible playing clubs all around the city. You will not find my name in any jazz dictionaries or discographies, or jazz books written by the likes of some authors such as Richard Sudhalter, Jim Collier, or Chip Deffaa, who incidentally wrote a book. I believe it was called, "Traditionalist and Revivalist" and on the cover was a picture of Vince Giordano.

CHAPTER THIRTEEN

The Song is Ended (The Melody Lingers On)

Basically, the book is about New York musicians. It was interesting to me that I have worked with most everyone in that book, and yet it is amazing that no one had mentioned me in all of the interviews. Even if it had only been by association, it would have been nice.

It saddens me to think that when I leave this world, musically, no one will ever know I was here. Except for my Mississippi Rag article written by Joe Klee, one of its writers for the New York area, or anyone who might read this book, although it is intended and written for my family.

The syndicated, "Jim Lowe and Friends" radio show was doing well and we produced a few CDs with the Smith Street Society Jazz Band. We did, "Live In New York, Vol. I and Vol 2," and one called "Jim Lowe, Who's Behind The Green Door" and another, "Salute to Dakota Staton" and finally our trombonist Herb Gardner came out with his CD called, "Ground Hog Day" with mostly original tunes.

One of the Jazz Festivals I enjoy doing each year is the Sackets Harbor Jazz Festival. The festival director is John H. Cleveland and it's put on by the Sackets Harbor Historical Society. It's a small festival but the whole town comes out for it plus, surrounding towns. The invited bands play at The Sentinel Bandstand which overlooks the great, Lake Ontario. It is a short ferry ride from Horne's Ferry nearby at Cape Vincent which will take you to Wolfe's Island, Canada.

The Speakeasy Jazz Band gets invited each year and the fourth

time is coming up in August of 2003. The band members have
been pretty consistent through the years and the regulars besides
myself on clarinet are John Bucher on cornet and Dick Dreiwitz
on trombone for the front line, and the rhythm section is Barbara
Dreiwitz on tuba and we use guest banjo players like Jimmy Mazzy
and Ken Salvo. It's a wonderful weekend. We start it off by playing
at The Tin Pan Galley Restaurant with a parade the following day
and then our concert later in the day.

Last year Canadian trombonist Rob McConnell was guest star
and he is a wonderful player and musician. He sat in with us when
we were playing at The Tin Pan Galley Restaurant. Other musicians
who are invited are people like Russ Kassoff on piano, bassist Linc
Milliman and vocalist Catherine Dupuis. It's a wonderful vacation
spot for anyone. It has a rich history. I can't wait to go back.

Now, to get back to Julie Wilson. As I mentioned, I would
keep you posted about the song I wrote for her called, "Julie." I
finally called her and asked if she ever got my song and she was
completely in the dark. It seems she is so unorganized that
somewhere in the clutter of all her unopened mail is my song. She
promised to look for it and told me how pleased she was and that
no one had ever written a song for her before. So for now we will
leave it at that.

The OKOM Label which the Smith Street Society Jazz Band
records for asked us to record with singer Dorothy Loudon who
had appeared on the Jim Lowe Show before. She has a wonderful
background as singer, actress, and Broadway Star. She is a good
jazz singer and we recorded with her at two different sessions on
August 6th and 7th, 2003 and got down enough tunes for a CD.
We put together a fine seven piece band for this one. The lineup
included Randy Reinhart on cornet, myself on clarinet/alto/soprano,
Herb Gardner on trombone, and the rhythm section included
Dick Voigt on piano, Barbara Dreiwitz on tuba, Robbie Scott on
drums and finally Bruce McNichols, banjo/guitar/Leader.

Before I forget again I failed to mention that none of the
recordings, and all the Jim Lowe and Friends radio shows would
not be possible if it wasn't for Mr. Bill Taggart who loves Our Kind

of Music and pays all the bills. He himself, as a youngster, played bass fiddle with jazz bands and eventually started his own successful business.

At this point in the book I think I've said all I want to say and to continue would be like keeping a daily journal and become boring. I would say if I had to do it all over again I probably would do it the same way as I have met some wonderful people along the way and made a few good friends whom I cherish, and I would not want that to change. I guess fame and fortune isn't everything and I think and hope I have brought a lot of pleasure with my music.

I'll end by quoting Joe Klee, writer for The Mississippi Rag, as he ended the article he did on me:

"Joe Licari has been known to refer to himself as, "The Invisible Clarinet Player." Perhaps the main reason for his anonymity is that he prefers to restrict his playing to the New York/New Jersey/New England area so he can have his family life and his career as well.

Once the outside world has been exposed by records or radio to Licari's ability on the Licari-ish stick, this "Invisible" musician will almost certainly become an imposing presence on the world's jazz scene.

CHAPTER FOURTEEN

THE FAMILY CHAPTER

For those of you who might want to know what has become of all our children over the years, I am happy to report the following:

Theresa, my oldest girl, is married to Tom Krawcuk. She graduated from SUNY, New Paltz, and just recently had her first child, a baby boy named Thomas the 3rd. They live in Florida, New York.

John, my second oldest, was married and is now divorced with no children. He is a successful salesman and lives in Boca Raton, Florida.

Marian, my third oldest, is married to Michael King. She graduated from Marymount College in Tarrytown, NY. She is a school teacher and has two small children, Max and Morgan. They live in New Windsor, New York.

Dominic, is my fourth oldest and is married to Lisa and they have a little girl named Kailyn. He has his own business and is a Window Contractor. He lives in Boca Raton, Florida.

Francis, a twin, is in the fifth position. He is single and recently graduated from Binghamton University of New York. He is job hunting and looking for something in the financial field. Presently, he is living in New City, New York.

David, the other twin, is also single and is the black sheep of the family. He is still trying to find himself. He presently lives in New City, New York.

Ann is my seventh child. She is married to Brendan Colligan and she will be graduating from St. Thomas Aquinas College with a teaching degree. She lives in Stony Point, New York.

Joe, Jr., my eighth child, is single and works for a large trailer park chain where he is employed as a maintenance man. He lives in Stony Point, New York.

Michael, my ninth child, is single. He learned a trade in the sheet metal business and he works for a big company. He lives in New City, New York.

Paul is the tenth child and the baby. He is still in high school and lives in New City, New York.

Valerie and I have been married to each other for 43 years. (Where did I go wrong?) Just kidding, and who knows what the future will bring. I hope it will be a lot more grandchildren for us as they are a joy and blessing—especially, when you don't have to take them home with you. (Just kidding.)

To my family, I hope you enjoy the book for what it is—a little bit about my life and what makes me the happiest, playing my music.

For my children and grandchildren, do what you enjoy in life that makes you happy, as you only go through this life once.

DISCOGRAPHY

The New Orleans Funeral and
Ragtime Orchestra

John Bucher-Cornet, Joe Licari—Clarinet, Dick Dreiwitz, Trombone,Barbara Dreiwitz, Tuba, Dick Miller, Piano, Mike Peters, Guitar, Jay Duke, Drums

Conn. Jazz Club, Meridan, Conn. Recorded on Feb. 21, 1976

Tune List

> Coquette
> Davenport Blues—CTJC-SLP 12

The Speakeasy Jazz Babies

John Bucher, Cornet, Joe Licari, Clarinet, Dick Dreiwitz, Trombone, Dick Miller, Piano, Marty Grosz, Guitar, Vocals, Barbara Dreiwitz, Tuba, Richie Barron, Drums, Betty Comora, Vocals

Conn. Jazz Club, Meridan, Conn. Recorded on Nov. 24, 1979

Tune List

> I've Got A Feeling I'm Falling
> I've Got My Fingers Crossed—CTJC-SLP 16

The Speakeasy Jazz Babies

John Bucher, Cornet, Joe Licari, Clarinet, Dick Dreiwitz, Trombone, Barbara Dreiwitz, Tuba, Dick Miller, Piano, Marty Grosz, Guitar,vocals, Carmen Mastren, Guitar, Richie Barron, Drums, Betty Comora, Vocals

DiGangi Studios, Recorded on Apr. 8,and May7, 1980

Tune List

> Side One
> Mahogany Hall Stomp
> I'm in The Market For You
> Save It Pretty Mama
> Hard Hearted Hannah
> Every Time I Fall In Love
> Once In Awhile
> Side Two
> Everybody Loves My Baby
> Do You Know What It Means To Miss New Orleans
> Doin' The New Lowdown
> The Love Nest
> From Monday On
> Limehouse Blues—SJB-100-LP

Natalie Lamb And Her Hot Quintet

Larry Weiss, Cornet, Joe Licari, Clarinet, Bruce Payne,Trombone, Dill Jones, Piano, Richie Barron, Drums. Natalie Lamb, Vocals and Leader

Conn. Jazz Club, Darien, Conn. Recorded on Sept,25, 1982

Tune List

> A Good Man is Hard To Find
> Lizzie Blues—CTJC-SLP-19

Joe Licari-That's A Plenty

Joe Licari, Clarinet, Leader, Jimmy Andrews, Piano, Chuck Slate, Drums

Watchung View Inn, Watchung, N.J.,Recorded on Dec. 9, 1984

Tune List

Royal Garden Blues
Ghost Of A Chance
Oh Lady Be Good
How Can You Face Me
Saint Louis Blues
That's A Plenty
Sweet Sue
Singing The Blues
Lazy River
Three Little Words—Clari1-101

The Speakeasy Jazz Babies in Concert

John Bucher, Cornet, Joe Licari, Clarinet, Dick Dreiwitz,Trombone, Barbara Dreiwitz, Tuba, Dick Miller, Piano. Marty Grosz, Banjo, Fred Stoll, Drums, Barbara Lea, Vocals

Long Island Trad. Society, Babylon, N.Y. Recorded on Dec. 8,1990

Tune List

Side A
Doctor Jazz
Winin' Boy Blues
Indiana
Tishomingo Blues
Riverboat Shuffle

Side B
Everybody Loves My Baby
A Kiss To Build A Dream On
'S Wonderful
Willie The Weeper
Once In A While—SJB-101-Cassette

Sweet And Hot With
The Red Onion Jazz Band

Larry Weiss, Cornet, Joe Licari, Clarinet, Alto Sax, Dick Dreiwitz, Trombone, Cynthia Sayer, Banjo, Hank Ross, Piano, Bob Sacchi, Tuba, Bass Sax, Bob Thompson, Drums, Leader

Watchung Arts Ctr., Watchung, N.J. Recorded on Apr. 21, 1995

Tune List

My Cabin Of Dreams
Blue Again
Ida, Sweet As Apple Cider
Oh! Sister Ain't That Hot
Black And Blue
Prof's Blues
That Da Da Strain
Lazy Bones
Saint James Infirmary
Don't Ever Change
Davenport Blues
Nauges
Sigh No More, My Ladies
A Handful Of Keyes
Panama—ROJB-101-CD

Big Apple Jazz Band {Big Apple Jam}

Warren Vache' Cornet, on tracks 1-3-6-8-10-11-12, Ed Polcer, Cornet, on tracks-2-4-5-7-9, Joe Licari, Clarinet, on all tracks, Tom Artin, Trombone, on all tracks, Leonard Gaskin, Bass, on tracks 2-4-5-7-9-, Dick Waldburger, Bass, on tracks 1-3-6-8-10-11-12, Giampaola Biagi, Drums, on all tracks, Dick Voigt, Piano, Leader, on all tracks, Stella Marrs, Vocal on track 4-only

Recorded Live at The Hopper House, Nyack, N.Y. Aug.5,1998-tracks 1-3-6-8-10-11-12

Recorded Live at The Helen Hayes Theater, Nyack,N.Y. Jan. 17,1999-tracks 2-4-5-7-9

Tune List

> Jubilee
> I Never Knew
> Blues my Naughty gives to me
> Mood Indigo
> Way Down Yonder in New Orleans
> New Orleans
> Ida
> Sweet Sue
> Tishomingo Blues
> Rosetta
> I've Got A Feeling I'm Falling—BAJB-100-CD

Jim Lowe And Company-Radio Show} "Salute To Dakota Staton

Jim Lowe, Piano and Host, Joe Licari, Clarinet

Part 1
Tony Bennett, Vocal, Smith Street Society Jazz Band, Dakota Staton, Vocal, Clayborne Cary, Vocal

Part 2
Frank Owens, Piano, Dakota Stanton, Vocal

Part 3
Pat Nicholas, Vocal, Dakota Staton, vocal

Part 4
Smith Street Society Jazz Band, Dakota Stanton, Interview

Part 5
Dakota Staton, Vocals

Recorded At The Museum of Television and Radio-New York City-Live, 1999

Tune List

>   Time On My Hands
>   Steppin Out With My Baby
>   I'm Looking Over A Four Leaf Clover
>   Anything Goes
>   Watchtower Magazine
>   I Should Care
>   September In The Rain
>   Gee Baby, Ain't I Good To You
>   Give Me The Simple Life
>   The, Late, Late Show
>   Misty
>   The Charleston
>   How Deep Is The Ocean
>   Jim
>   The, Late, Late Show—OKOM Show 91-CD

The Smith Street Society Jazz Band—
Live In New York Vol, 1

Joe Licari, Clarinet, Dick Voigt, Piano, Barbara Dreiwitz, Tuba, Rocco Patierno, Trombone, Vocals, Bruce McNicholas, Banjo, vocals And Leader

Triad Supper Club, New York City, Recorded Live-1999

Tune List

Alexander's Ragtime Band
Goody, Goody
Yes Sir, That's My Baby
Margie
Muskrat Ramble
We'll Build A Bungalow
That's A Plenty
Frankie And Johnny
Avalon
Jersey Bounce
You're Nobody, Till Somebody Loves You
Wrap Your Trouble in Dreams
Ballin The Jack
A Shanty in Old Shanty Town
When My Sugar Walks Down The Street
Peoria
Jazz Me Blues
Sweet Georgia Brown {Buddy Greco}-Vocal
The Green Door {Jim Lowe} Vocal—Okom-1-1036-CD

The Smith Street Society Jazz Band—
Live in New York, Vol,2

Joe Licari, Clarinet, Herb Gardner, Trombone, Dick Voigt, Piano, Barbara Dreiwitz, Tuba, Bruce McNicholas, Banjo, Vocals, Leader

Tune List

>Bill Bailey, Won't You Please Come Home
>The Aba Daba Honeymoon
>Back Home In Indiana
>Coney Island Washboard
>Butter And Egg Man
>Scotch and Soda
>By The Beautiful Sea
>The Japanese Sandman
>The Darktowen Strutters Ball
>When The Saints Come Marching In
>Borneo
>I Double Dare You
>Some Of These Days
>Charley, My Boy
>Only You
>After You've Gone{Dorothy Loudon} Vocal
>Is It True What They Say About Dixie {Dorothy Loudon}
>   Vocal
>Senior Moments{Kay Ballard} Vocal
>Hard Hearted Hannah _Jim Lowe and Mark Nadler}
>   Vocals—OKOM-1-1037-CD

Jim Lowe-Who's Behind The Green Door??

Joe Licari, Clarinet, Barbara Dreiwitz, Tuba, Dick Voigt,Piano, on tracks 3-6-8-9-11-12, Rocco Patierno, Trombone, Bruce McNicolas,Banjo,Drums, Herb Gardner, Trombone, Piano, on track 1, Jim Lowe, Piano, Vocal, Leader,on tracks2-4-5-7-10-13-14-15

Recorded at Museum Of Television and Radio—New York City-Live-2000

Tune List

Back Home In Indiana
What Can I Say After I say I'm Sorry
Dinah
My Shining Hour
The Hamptons
Birth Of The Blues
I Don't Want To Set The World On Fire
Oh Lady Be Good
Way Down Yonder In New Orleans
Moon Song
It's Delovely
Mean To Me
I've Got A Feeling I'm Falling
That Old Feeling
Network Radio Medley—Okom-1023-CD

Herb Gardner-Groundhog Day

Tracks 1-4-6-8-10-13-21, Herb Gardner, Trombone,Vocals, Leader, Bruce McNicholas,Banjo, Joe Licari, Clarinet, Soprano Sax, Dick Voigt, Piano, Barbara,Dreiwitz, Tuba, Track 8, Rocco Patierno, Trombone, Track 17, Noel Kalestsky, Sop, Sax Dick Dreiwitz, Trombone Track 18, Herb Gardner, Trombone, Keyboards, Percussion, Tracks 15-23, Hank Ross, Piano, Joe Licari, Clarinet, Sop, Sax. Tracks 2-3-5-11-14-22, Herb Gardner, Trombone, Piano, Drums and Vocal,Bruce McNicholas, Banjo, Guitar

Tracks 9-12-19-20-24, Joe Hanchow, Tuba, Bass, Tracks7-16, Mike Peters, Banjo, Vince Giordano, Drums, Track 7—Bruce McNicholas, Sop. Sax

Vocal Trio-Bruce McNicholas, Lynne Mc Nicholas, Herb Gardner

Tune List

Groundhog's Day
Staten Island
I Believe In Miracles
Sweet And Slow
Summah People
Sugar Babe I'm Leaven'
Fiery Horse
Mama Woncha' Please Come Homer?
Yonz Gonz Galookis'
After You've Gone
Jazzbeaux's Time Of Night
Your Morning Man
Let's Misbehave
So Who's Gonna Know?
Seventh Heaven
Big Brother Stomp
She Looks Like Helen Brown
That Lonely Day
Nabob
Rich Conaty'
Only You
These Are The Good Old Days
What A Day!
Forties In The Eighties—OKOM-1052-CD Recorded-
   2000

Haunting Melody

Joe Licari, Clarinet, Larry Weiss, Piano

Sully's Studio, South Bound Brook, N.J., Recorded on
July,30,2002 and February,13, 2003

Tune List

As Long As I Live
Memories Of You
Emaline
Larry's Tune
Haunting Melody
Where Or When
Prof's Blues
I Never Knew
Poor Butterfly/ Embraceable You
On The Alamo
Moonlight Becomes You
Little Things Mean So Much
Gone With The Wind
I've Got A crush On You
Rosetta
Haunting Melody
Row About You
All Too Soon—Clari1-102-CD

INDEX